National Geographic Kids **Ultimate**

U.S. ROAD TRIP

Atlas 2nd EDITION

Maps, games, ACTIVITIES, and more for hours of backseat fun!

NATIONAL GEOGRAPHIC
WASHINGTON, D.C.

TABLE OF CONTENTS

HOW TO USE THIS ATLAS

STATE FACTS
For the names of state birds, flowers, and animals or trees, look above the state name.

STATE NICKNAME
Do you know your state's nickname? Every state has one! You'll find it below each state name.

INTRODUCTION
The introductory paragraph offers a fun overview of each state.

TRAFFIC LAWS/ SILLY SIGNS/ FANTASTIC FACTS
Throughout the book, we've included the wackiest laws, the silliest signs, or the most fantastic facts we could find. Look for them on each spread.

ROADSIDE ATTRACTIONS
For fun, wacky, and wild side trip ideas, eyeball the list of Roadside Attractions.

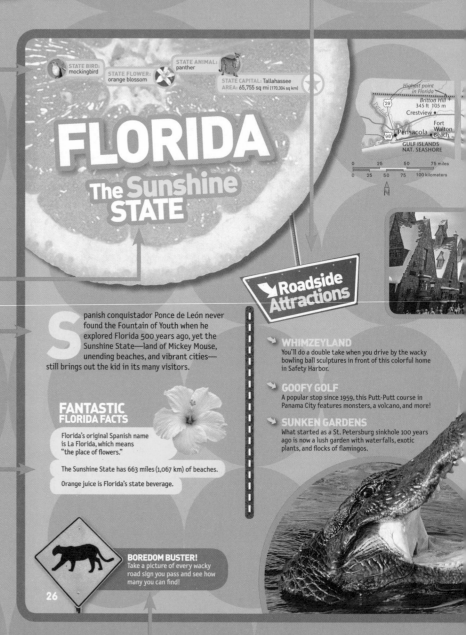

STATE BIRD: mockingbird
STATE FLOWER: orange blossom
STATE ANIMAL: panther
STATE CAPITAL: Tallahassee
AREA: 65,755 sq mi (170,304 sq km)

Highest point in Florida
Britton Hill
345 ft 105 m
Crestview
29
98 Pensacola Fort Walton Beach
GULF ISLANDS NAT. SEASHORE
0 25 50 75 miles
0 25 50 75 100 kilometers

FLORIDA
The Sunshine STATE

Roadside Attractions

S panish conquistador Ponce de León never found the Fountain of Youth when he explored Florida 500 years ago, yet the Sunshine State—land of Mickey Mouse, unending beaches, and vibrant cities—still brings out the kid in its many visitors.

FANTASTIC FLORIDA FACTS
Florida's original Spanish name is La Florida, which means "the place of flowers."

The Sunshine State has 663 miles (1,067 km) of beaches.

Orange juice is Florida's state beverage.

WHIMZEYLAND
You'll do a double take when you drive by the wacky bowling ball sculptures in front of this colorful home in Safety Harbor.

GOOFY GOLF
A popular stop since 1959, this Putt-Putt course in Panama City features monsters, a volcano, and more!

SUNKEN GARDENS
What started as a St. Petersburg sinkhole 100 years ago is now a lush garden with waterfalls, exotic plants, and flocks of flamingos.

BOREDOM BUSTER!
Take a picture of every wacky road sign you pass and see how many you can find!

26

BOREDOM BUSTER/GPS BOREDOM BUSTER
For nonstop fun on your road trip, go to the boredom busters. These features ask you to use a camera or phone to take pictures, a smartphone to look up information, or a GPS to find locations or landmarks.

MAP

To find all the locations mentioned on the page, check out the map! Then look for state capitals, highways, bodies of water, and even national parks.

5 COOL THINGS

These are the five places you must visit while in the state! Follow the pointers from each picture to the map to find out exactly where these cool places are located. Then hit the road!

MAP KEY

- • Aspen .... *town of under 25,000 residents*
- • Frankfort .... *town of 25,000 to 99,999*
- • **San Jose** .... *city of 100,000 to 999,999*
- • **New York** .... *city of 1,000,000 and over*
- ⊛ National capital
- ⊛ State capital
- ◻ Fort
- ◻ Point of interest
- + Mountain peak with elevation above sea level
- • Low point with elevation below sea level
- ⸺ Limited access highway
- ⸺ Other highway
- --- Auto ferry

- 🛡80 🛡40 Interstate highway number
- 🛡50 Federal highway number
- ⬡20 State highway number
- ⬡30 Foreign highway number
- --- Trail
- ••••• State or national boundary
- ••••• Continental divide
- ⸺ River
- --- Intermittent river
- ⊢⊢⊢ Canal
- Lake and dam
- Intermittent lake
- Dry lake
- Swamp
- Glacier
- Sand
- Lava
- Area below sea level
- Indian Reservation, **IND. RES., I.R.**
- State Park, **S.P.**
  State Historical Park, **S.H.P.**
  State Historic Site, **S.H.S.**
- National Battlefield, **N.B.**
  National Battlefield Park, **N.B.P.**
  National Battlefield Site, **N.B.S.**
  National Historic Landmark
  National Historic Site, **N.H.S.**
  National Historical Area, **N.H.A.**
  National Historical Park, **N.H.P.**
  National Lakeshore
  National Landmark
  National Military Park, **N.M.P.**
  National Memorial, **NAT. MEM.**
  National Monument, **NAT. MON., N.M.**
  National Park, **NAT. PK., N.P.**
  National Parkway
  National Preserve
  National Recreation Area, **N.R.A.**
  National River
  National Riverway
  National Scenic Area
  National Seashore
  National Volcanic Monument
- National Forest, **NAT. FOR., N.F.**
- National Grassland, **N.G.**
- National Wildlife Refuge, **N.W.R.**
  National Conservation Area, **N.C.A.**
- National Marine Sanctuary, **N.M.S.**

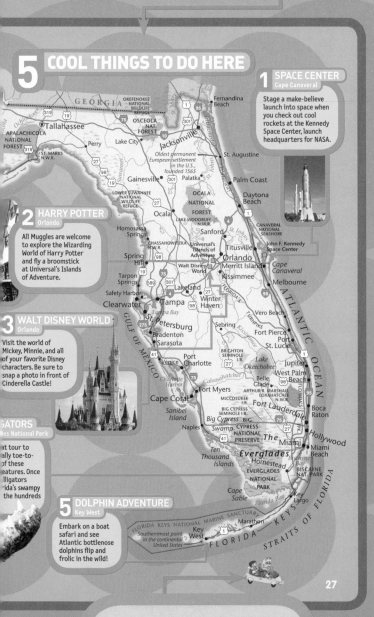

5 COOL THINGS TO DO HERE

1 SPACE CENTER
Cape Canaveral

Stage a make-believe launch into space when you check out cool rockets at the Kennedy Space Center, launch headquarters for NASA.

2 HARRY POTTER
Orlando

All Muggles are welcome to explore the Wizarding World of Harry Potter and fly a broomstick at Universal's Islands of Adventure.

3 WALT DISNEY WORLD
Orlando

Visit the world of Mickey, Minnie, and all of your favorite Disney characters. Be sure to snap a photo in front of Cinderella Castle!

GATORS
les National Park

at tour to ally toe-to- of these eatures. Once lligators rida's swampy the hundreds

5 DOLPHIN ADVENTURE
Key West

Embark on a boat safari and see Atlantic bottlenose dolphins flip and frolic in the wild!

27

AUNT BERTHA

Meet Aunt Bertha. You'll find her speeding through various pages inside this book. Count how many times she appears and then check the answer key on page 135 to see if you're right!

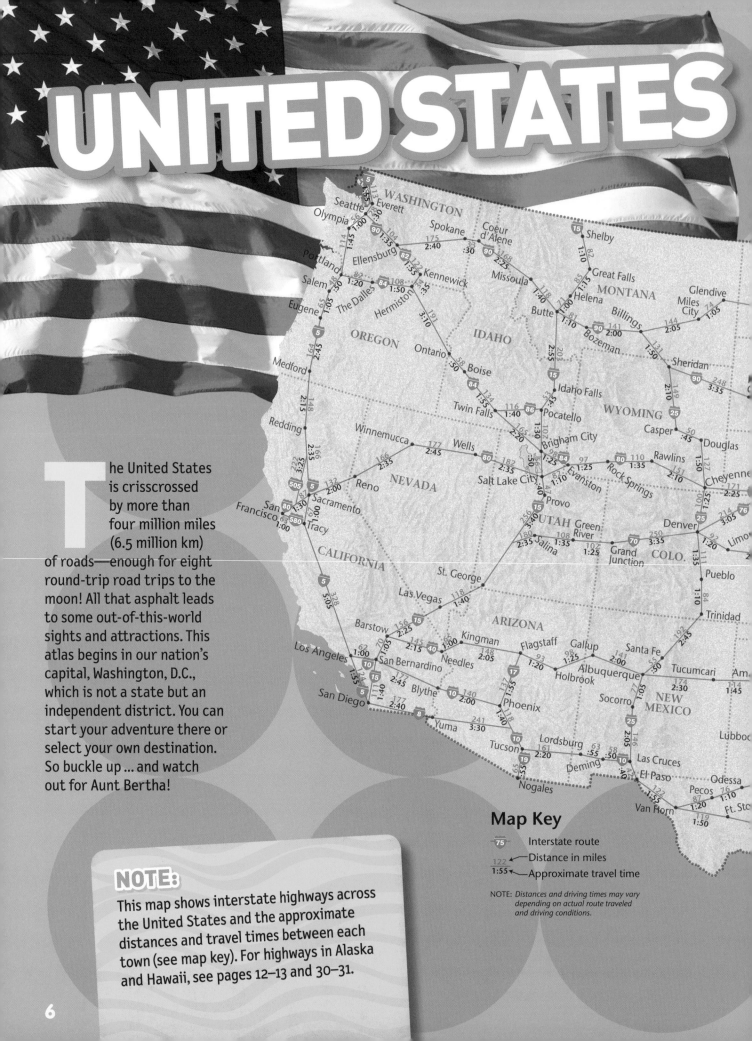

UNITED STATES

T he United States is crisscrossed by more than four million miles (6.5 million km) of roads—enough for eight round-trip road trips to the moon! All that asphalt leads to some out-of-this-world sights and attractions. This atlas begins in our nation's capital, Washington, D.C., which is not a state but an independent district. You can start your adventure there or select your own destination. So buckle up ... and watch out for Aunt Bertha!

Map Key

<u>75</u> — Interstate route

<u>122</u> — Distance in miles
1:55 — Approximate travel time

NOTE: *Distances and driving times may vary depending on actual route traveled and driving conditions.*

NOTE:

This map shows interstate highways across the United States and the approximate distances and travel times between each town (see map key). For highways in Alaska and Hawaii, see pages 12–13 and 30–31.

WASHINGTON, D.C.

Our Nation's CAPITAL

Roadside Attractions

Welcome to America's capital, a city full of must-see museums and monuments. Named for George Washington in 1791, the home of the federal government crams an entire state's worth of historic attractions into the president's backyard.

FANTASTIC
WASHINGTON, D.C. FACTS

It might be the capital of the United States, but Washington, D.C., isn't part of any single state. It's an independent federal district.

Think your local library has a lot of books? The Library of Congress has more than 800 miles (1,287 km) of bookshelves!

The president's home wasn't officially called the White House until 1901. Before that it held several names, including the President's Palace.

BOREDOM BUSTER!
The Washington Monument is one of D.C.'s most visited sights. Towering more than 555 feet (169 m) in the air, it's also one of the city's tallest structures. Lie on your back and point your camera up for a fun shot!

MADAME TUSSAUDS
The D.C. branch of the famous wax museum lets you meet every U.S. president—or at least their eerily lifelike wax incarnations.

THE MANSION ON O STREET
Take a self-guided tour through more than 100 rooms and 70 secret doors in this historic building. The mansion is also a hotel, so it's a cool place to stay, too!

NATIONAL GEOGRAPHIC MUSEUM
Expeditions and adventure stories come to life at the National Geographic Society's base of operations.

2 GIANT PANDAS
National Zoo

Only about 1,800 of these magnificent black-and-white bears are left in the world. Meet some of them at this famous zoo.

3 MUSEUM OF NATURAL HISTORY
National Mall

Get lost in the history of life at this world-famous museum, home to dino bones, woolly mammoths, and ancient treasures from many cultures.

5 COOL THINGS TO DO HERE

Potomac
270
97
29
495
95
495
355
185
Silver Spring
Bethesda
1
MD VA.
495
MD D.C.
MD D.C.
29
Area Enlarged Below
267
123
50
Washington, D.C.
7
295
29
Arlington
66
50
214
95
495
29
237
50
7
Suitland
50
495
244
1
295
4
Annandale
236
7
5
Alexandria
0   2 mi
395
95
95
495
210
0   3 km
27
400

1 AIR & SPACE MUSEUM
National Mall

Take a voyage through the evolution of flight—from the Wright brothers' rickety first airplane to the Apollo 11 moon module—at this out-of-this-world Smithsonian museum.

MAP KEY

- ☐ National Historic Site, N.H.S.
- ☐ Point of interest
- ▬ Limited access highway
- ▬ Other road

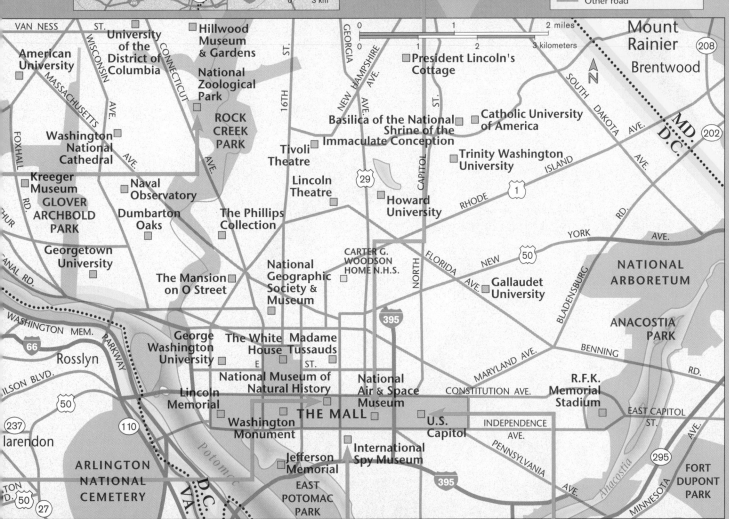

VAN NESS ST.
University of the District of Columbia
Hillwood Museum & Gardens
American University
National Zoological Park
GEORGIA
President Lincoln's Cottage
Mount Rainier
208
Brentwood
WISCONSIN AVE.
CONNECTICUT
ROCK CREEK PARK
16TH ST.
NEW HAMPSHIRE AVE.
Basilica of the National Shrine of the Immaculate Conception
CAPITOL ST.
Catholic University of America
SOUTH DAKOTA AVE.
MD D.C.
202
FOXHALL
Washington National Cathedral
MASSACHUSETTS AVE.
Tivoli Theatre
Trinity Washington University
ISLAND
Kreeger Museum
GLOVER ARCHBOLD PARK
Naval Observatory
Lincoln Theatre
29
Howard University
RHODE
1
RD.
Dumbarton Oaks
The Phillips Collection
YORK AVE.
NATIONAL ARBORETUM
Georgetown University
CANAL RD.
The Mansion on O Street
National Geographic Society & Museum
CARTER G. WOODSON HOME N.H.S.
NORTH
FLORIDA AVE.
NEW
50
Gallaudet University
BLADENSBURG
ANACOSTIA PARK
WASHINGTON MEM. PARKWAY
66
Rosslyn
George Washington University
The White House
Madame Tussauds
E ST.
395
MARYLAND AVE.
BENNING
R.F.K. Memorial Stadium
RD.
EAST CAPITOL ST.
WILSON BLVD.
50
Lincoln Memorial
National Museum of Natural History
National Air & Space Museum
THE MALL
CONSTITUTION AVE.
295
237
Clarendon
110
Washington Monument
U.S. Capitol
INDEPENDENCE AVE.
FORT DUPONT PARK
ARLINGTON NATIONAL CEMETERY
Jefferson Memorial
International Spy Museum
PENNSYLVANIA AVE.
Anacostia
MINNESOTA AVE.
27
D.C. VA.
EAST POTOMAC PARK
395

0   1   2 miles
0   1   2   3 kilometers

4 SECRET GADGETS
International Spy Museum

Learn the art of espionage and play with high-tech spy gizmos, including button-size cameras and invisible ink.

5 U.S. CAPITOL
National Mall

Stroll the hallowed corridors of America's political heart—and listen for errant whispers in the acoustically wacky Statuary Hall.

ALABAMA

The Heart of DIXIE

STATE BIRD: yellowhammer

STATE TREE: southern longleaf pine

STATE FLOWER: camellia

STATE CAPITAL: Montgomery

AREA: 52,419 sq mi (135,765 sq km)

I f you're searching for soft, white sand beaches and warm turquoise waters, Alabama could be the ticket! This scenic state is also known for its Southern hospitality and tangy barbecue, as well as for its civil rights legacy and role in the space program.

FANTASTIC ALABAMA FACTS

Bear wrestling is illegal in Alabama.

It's illegal to pretend to be a nun or priest in Alabama.

It's against the law to take a bath in Mobile's fountains.

5 COOL THINGS TO DO HERE

1 SPACE CAMP
Huntsville

Prepare for liftoff with a six-day crash course in astronautics at the U.S. Space and Rocket Center, which built the rockets that took us to the moon.

Roadside Attractions

➤ U.S. ARMY AVIATION MUSEUM
A heaven for helicopter lovers, this Fort Rucker museum displays some 50 aircraft—from early prototypes to state-of-the-art gunships.

➤ UNCLAIMED BAGGAGE CENTER
The world's lost airport luggage is found at this unusual Scottsboro store—and you can buy it! Browse miles of shelves crammed with gadgets, toys, and other unclaimed treasures.

➤ STATUE OF LIBERTY
If you can't make it to New York City to see the real deal, this one-fifth-size reproduction is a marvel in miniature.

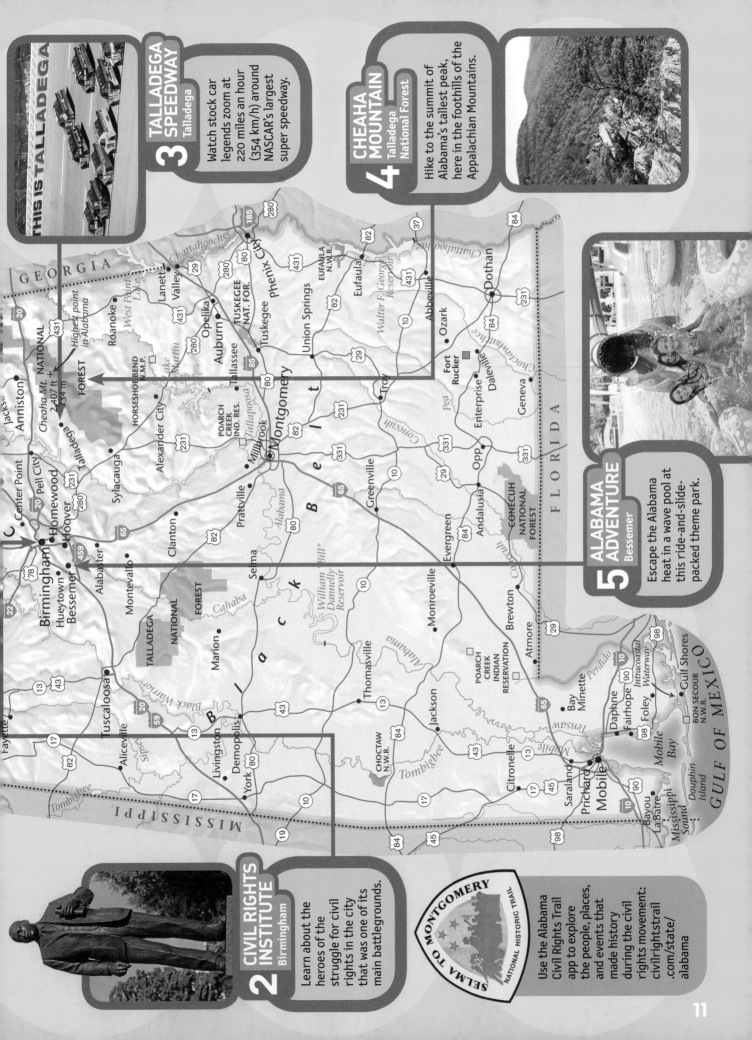

THIS IS TALLADEGA

3 TALLADEGA SPEEDWAY
Talladega

Watch stock car legends zoom at 220 miles an hour (354 km/h) around NASCAR's largest super speedway.

4 CHEAHA MOUNTAIN
Talladega National Forest

Hike to the summit of Alabama's tallest peak, here in the foothills of the Appalachian Mountains.

5 ALABAMA ADVENTURE
Bessemer

Escape the Alabama heat in a wave pool at this ride-and-slide-packed theme park.

2 CIVIL RIGHTS INSTITUTE
Birmingham

Learn about the heroes of the struggle for civil rights in the city that was one of its main battlegrounds.

SELMA TO MONTGOMERY
NATIONAL HISTORIC TRAIL

Use the Alabama Civil Rights Trail app to explore the people, places, and events that made history during the civil rights movement: civilrightstrail.com/state/alabama

GEORGIA

FLORIDA

MISSISSIPPI

GULF OF MEXICO

Highest point in Alabama
Cheaha Mt. 2,407 ft + 734 m

CHEAHA MT. NATIONAL FOREST

TALLADEGA NATIONAL FOREST

CONECUH NATIONAL FOREST

HORSESHOE BEND N.M.P.

TUSKEGEE NAT. FOR.

POARCH CREEK IND. RES.

POARCH CREEK INDIAN RESERVATION

CHOCTAW N.W.R.

EUFAULA N.W.R.

BON SECOUR N.W.R.

Black Belt

STATE BIRD: willow ptarmigan

STATE FLOWER: forget-me-not

STATE ANIMAL: moose

STATE CAPITAL: Juneau
AREA: 663,267 sq mi (1,717,862 sq km)

ALASKA
The Last Frontier STATE

1 ALASKA RAILROAD TOUR
Denali National Park

Watch grizzly bears, caribou, and moose whiz by as you ride the rails past this majestic national park dominated by Denali (Mount McKinley), North America's tallest peak.

Calling Alaska big is like saying water is wet. The 49th state is more than twice the size of the second largest, Texas. From its towering terrain to its 10-foot (3-m) Kodiak bears, everything in Alaska is epic.

Roadside Attractions

FANTASTIC ALASKA FACTS

America's northernmost, westernmost, and easternmost points by longitude are all in Alaska.

Alaskan fishermen have one of the most dangerous jobs in America.

Barrow, Alaska, goes through three months of daylight in the summer and two months of darkness in the winter.

ALASKA RAPTOR CENTER

Injured bald eagles, owls, and falcons get a second chance at this rehab facility for rescued birds of prey in Sitka.

EL DORADO GOLD MINE

This working mine near Fairbanks is a mother lode of Alaskan gold-mining history. Visiting prospectors can even pan for gold!

TOTEM HERITAGE CENTER

This museum in Ketchikan preserves ornate 19th-century totem poles from native Alaskan villages.

CHUKCHI SEA

ALASKA MARITIME N.W.R.

KRUSE NA MON

RUSSIA

Bering Strait

only 2.5 miles from Russia

Little Diomede I.

BERI LAND BR NAT. PRE

Taylor

Teller

Sev Peni

St. Lawrence Island

Nome

Nor Sou

Yukon Delta

Emmonak

Mountain Village

Hooper Bay

YUKON DELTA

St. Matthew I.

ALASKA MARITIME N.W.R.

Nelson I.

NATIONA

WILDLIFE

RE

Nunivak I.

BERING SEA

St. Paul

Pribilof Islands

ALASKA MARITIME N.W.R.

Attu I.

NEAR IS.

Agattu I.

A L E U T I A N

A L A S K A

RAT ISLANDS

Kiska I.

Amchitka I.

Semisopochnoi Island

Garcloi I.

Tanaga I.

Adak I.

ANDREANOF ISLANDS

Atka I.

Amlia I.

Seguam I.

Yunaska I.

Islands of Four Mountains

Umnak I.

Unalaska I.

Dutch Harbor

Unalaska

I S L A N D S

M A R I T I M E   N A T I O N A L   W I L D L I F E   R E F U G E

IZEMBEK N.W.R.

Unimak I.

Alas

ALASKA

Sanak I.

0   100   200 miles

0   100   200   300 kilomete

GPS BOREDOM BUSTER!
Much of Alaska is reachable only by boat or plane. Use your GPS to see where you can go by road and where you can't.

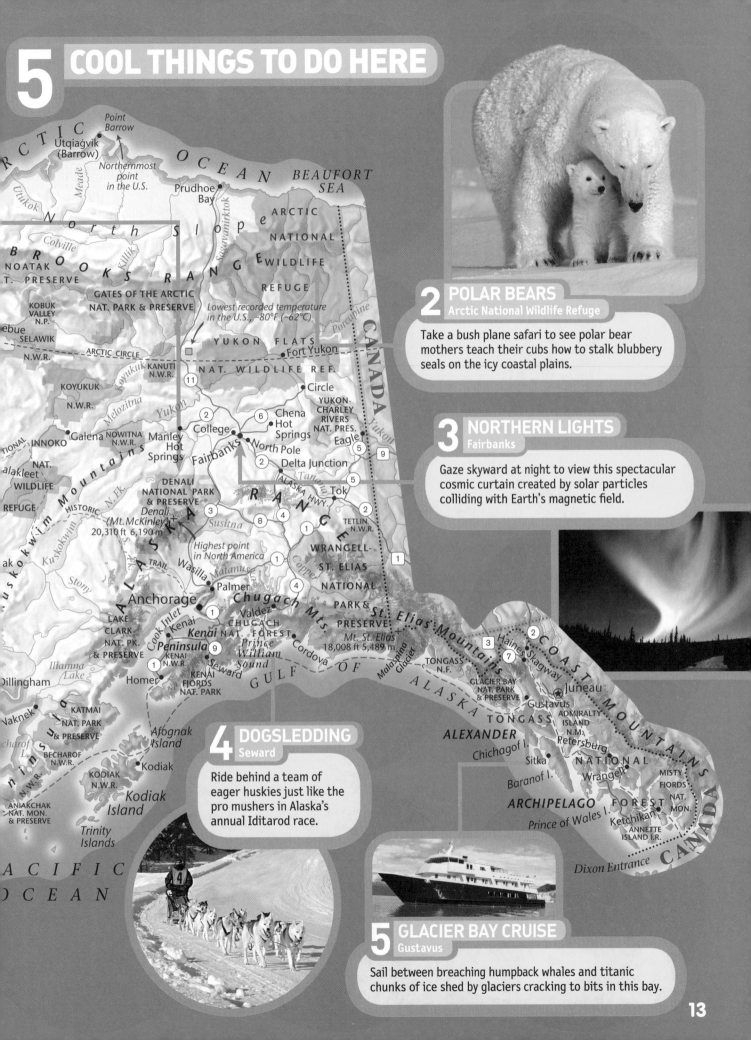

5 COOL THINGS TO DO HERE

2 POLAR BEARS
Arctic National Wildlife Refuge

Take a bush plane safari to see polar bear mothers teach their cubs how to stalk blubbery seals on the icy coastal plains.

3 NORTHERN LIGHTS
Fairbanks

Gaze skyward at night to view this spectacular cosmic curtain created by solar particles colliding with Earth's magnetic field.

4 DOGSLEDDING
Seward

Ride behind a team of eager huskies just like the pro mushers in Alaska's annual Iditarod race.

5 GLACIER BAY CRUISE
Gustavus

Sail between breaching humpback whales and titanic chunks of ice shed by glaciers cracking to bits in this bay.

ARIZONA
The Grand Canyon STATE

STATE BIRD: cactus wren

STATE FLOWER: saguaro cactus blossom

STATE ANIMAL: ringtail cat

STATE CAPITAL: Phoenix

AREA: 113,998 sq mi (295,256 sq km)

Your eyeballs and brain will have a disconnect when you visit Arizona, a land of mind-boggling heights and unreal lowlands. The first time you peer over the rim of the Grand Canyon, the state's greatest natural treasure, you won't believe your eyes.

Roadside Attractions

ROOSTER COGBURN OSTRICH RANCH

You've never been to a petting zoo like this one in Picacho! Visitors can feed the ranch's big birds by hand. (Don't worry—ostriches don't have teeth.)

METEOR CRATER

An asteroid smacked into the desert near Winslow 50,000 years ago; today it's a nearly mile-wide (1,200-m) tourist attraction full of trails and interactive exhibits.

BIOSPHERE 2

Scientists in the 1990s sealed themselves into this enclosed ecosystem near Tucson to study humanity's effect on the environment. Today you can tour its artificial rainforest, coral reef, and desert habitats.

5 COOL THINGS TO DO HERE

1 GRAND CANYON SKYWALK
Grand Canyon West

Walk where eagles soar along this glass-bottomed sidewalk perched 4,000 feet (1.2 km) above the floor of the Grand Canyon, one of the natural wonders of the world.

2 TRAIL RIDE
Monument Valley

Mount up for a wild ride among flattop buttes and mesas made famous by countless Westerns.

FANTASTIC ARIZONA FACTS

Camels were once imported from the Middle East to carry goods across Arizona for the U.S. Army.

Arizona has more land set aside for Native Americans than any other state.

Unlike most of the U.S., Arizona doesn't observe daylight saving time. You'll be an hour ahead if you visit during the summer!

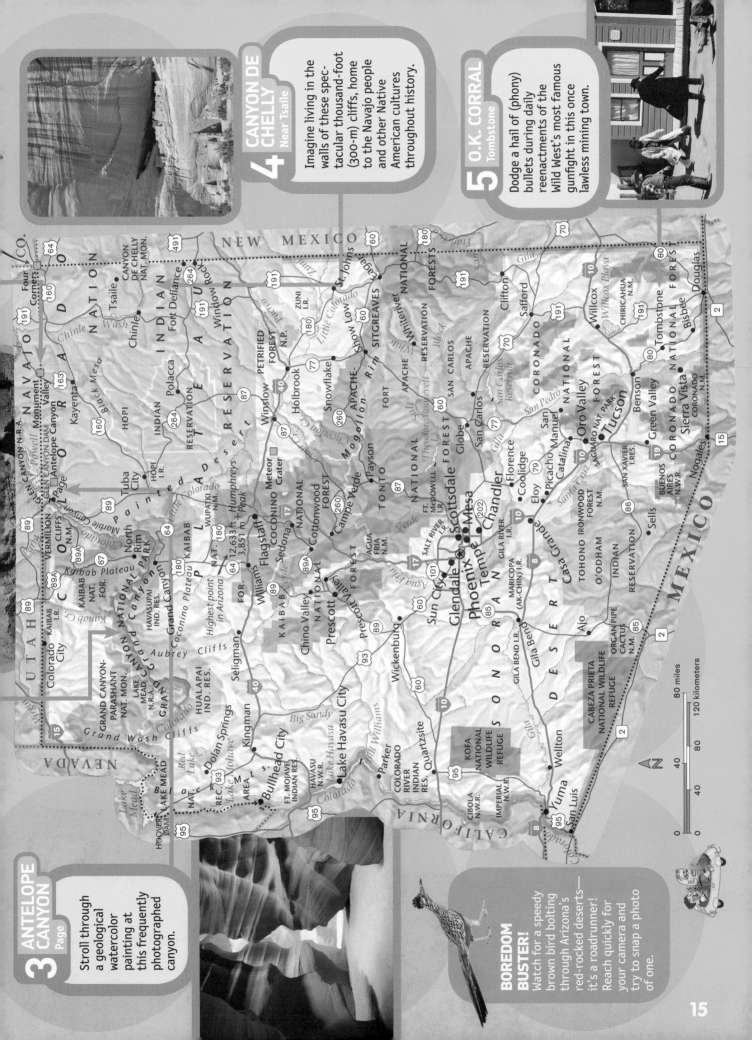

3 ANTELOPE CANYON
Page

Stroll through a geological watercolor painting at this frequently photographed canyon.

4 CANYON DE CHELLY
Near Tsaile

Imagine living in the walls of these spectacular thousand-foot (300-m) cliffs, home to the Navajo people and other Native American cultures throughout history.

5 O.K. CORRAL
Tombstone

Dodge a hail of (phony) bullets during daily reenactments of the Wild West's most famous gunfight in this once lawless mining town.

BOREDOM BUSTER!
Watch for a speedy brown bird bolting through Arizona's red-rocked deserts—it's a roadrunner! Reach quickly for your camera and try to snap a photo of one.

15

5 COOL THINGS TO DO HERE

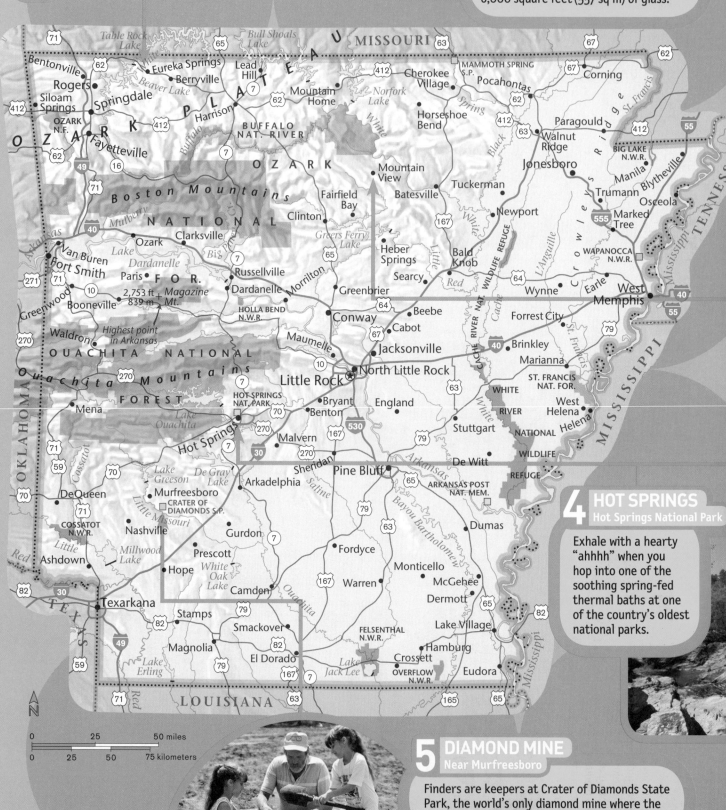

1 THORNCROWN CHAPEL
near Eureka Springs

Nestled in the Ozarks and rising 48 feet (14.6 m) into the sky, Thorncrown Chapel is made up of 425 windows and more than 6,000 square feet (557 sq m) of glass.

4 HOT SPRINGS
Hot Springs National Park

Exhale with a hearty "ahhhh" when you hop into one of the soothing spring-fed thermal baths at one of the country's oldest national parks.

5 DIAMOND MINE
Near Murfreesboro

Finders are keepers at Crater of Diamonds State Park, the world's only diamond mine where the public can prospect for precious stones.

STATE BIRD: mockingbird

STATE FLOWER: apple blossom

STATE ANIMAL: white-tailed deer

STATE CAPITAL: Little Rock
AREA: 53,179 sq mi (137,732 sq km)

ARKANSAS

The Natural STATE

2 LOCO ROPES TREETOP ADVENTURE
Mountain View

Dangle dozens of feet in the air as you hop from platform to platform and tiptoe on tightropes at this high-wire adventure park.

3 MAGIC SPRINGS
Hot Springs

Break a sweat on this theme park's twisting coasters before cooling off in its water park.

For outdoor enthusiasts, Arkansas is a full-service destination. Its rugged Ozark Plateau is a mountainous playground for hikers, campers, and mountain bikers, who can cap off their strenuous excursions with a soothing soak in the state's many natural hot springs.

FANTASTIC ARKANSAS FACTS

Nine million gallons (34 million L) of water flow through Mammoth Spring State Park each hour.

Arkansas' name came from the Quapaw Indians, whom the French called the "Arkansaw."

Arkansas is the only U.S. state that actively mines diamonds.

Roadside Attractions

BIG CAT REFUGE
Abandoned lions, tigers, and even a bear roam their new homes at Turpentine Creek Wildlife Refuge in Eureka Springs.

BLANCHARD SPRINGS CAVERNS
Spelunk a newly opened section of this cave system in Mountain View to reach a cluster of towering subterranean columns appropriately named the Titans.

WWII SUBMARINE
Ponder life at sea in an oversize sardine can when you tour the still working U.S.S. *Razorback* at North Little Rock's Inland Maritime Museum.

BOREDOM BUSTER!
Former president Bill Clinton was born in Arkansas. Use your camera to snap pictures of Clinton-themed roadside stops and see how many you can find!

CALIFORNIA

The Golden STATE

STATE BIRD: California quail

STATE FLOWER: golden poppy

STATE ANIMAL: California grizzly bear

STATE CAPITAL: Sacramento
AREA: 163,696 sq mi (423,972 sq km)

F rom its scorching deserts to its snowcapped mountains, California is a state of extremes. The southern half is home to Hollywood and surf culture. Coastal redwoods in the north tower to dizzying heights. This state got its nickname from the discovery of gold there in 1848. California is also home to fields of golden poppy flowers that bloom each spring.

FANTASTIC CALIFORNIA FACTS

In Carmel-by-the-Sea, it's illegal to place chairs on public sidewalks or parking lots for the purpose of eating from them.

In the city of Baldwin Park, it's illegal to ride your bike in a public park.

Dogs are not allowed to dig holes in dog parks in Los Angeles County.

Roadside Attractions

MONOPOLY IN THE PARK
In San Jose, near the Children's Discovery Center in Guadalupe River Park and Gardens, you'll find the largest permanent outdoor Monopoly game board. It even set a Guinness world record!

CABAZON DINOSAURS
It took about 10 years to build Dinny the *Apatosaurus*. Her 150-foot (46-m) body hides a gift shop that you can visit through a door in her tail!

QUEEN CALIFIA'S MAGICAL CIRCLE GARDEN
This wacky garden in Escondido features vibrant, colorful, whimsical sculptures of giant reptiles and mythical beasts.

5 COOL THINGS TO DO HERE

1 REDWOODS
Crescent City

Pitch a tent among towering redwoods that started as saplings a thousand years ago.

BOREDOM BUSTER!
Take pictures of all the cool things you see as you ride along in the car and then make your own map of your California road trip.

2 POINT LOBOS
Carmel

Splash and splash in tide pools or at the beach at Point Lobos State Natural Reserve in Carmel Highlands.

3 SAND DUNES
Death Valley

Hike among the sunny dunes of North America's hottest desert.

4 UNIVERSAL STUDIOS
Los Angeles

Ride roaring roller coasters based on Hollywood blockbusters.

5 SAN DIEGO ZOO
San Diego

Say hello to thousands of animals—from peacocks to pandas—at one of the world's largest zoos.

19

STATE BIRD: lark bunting

STATE FLOWER: Rocky Mountain columbine

 STATE ANIMAL: Rocky Mountain bighorn sheep

STATE CAPITAL: Denver
AREA: 103,730 sq mi (269,659 sq km)

COLORADO

The Centennial STATE

f Colorado's breathtaking Rocky Mountain scenery doesn't make your head spin, the thin air will! With 54 peaks towering above 14,000 feet (4.3 km), Colorado is the tallest state in the country. So why is it called the Centennial State? Colorado became a state 100 years after the Declaration of Independence was signed.

TRAFFIC LAWS YOU WON'T BELIEVE

Better become an expert skier before visiting Vail. It's illegal to crash into lift towers, signs, and any equipment on the slopes and trails!

Firing a catapult on Aspen's streets is against the law.

You're not allowed to roll boulders on the streets of Boulder!

Roadside Attractions

U.S. MINT
This U.S. government moneymaking factory in Denver mints a whole mountain range of spare change—some 40 million coins a day!

UFO WATCHTOWER
The owner of this two-story platform in the San Luis Valley—a UFO hot spot—invites passersby to stop and watch the skies for alien visitors.

GARDEN OF THE GODS
Towering formations of red sandstone frame the distant snowcapped peaks of the Rocky Mountains at this geological wonderland near Colorado Springs.

1 DINOSAUR FOSSILS
Dinosaur National Monument

Count the dinosaur bones embedded in a cliff face inside the Dinosaur Quarry Visitor Center on the Utah border.

3 VAIL
Vail

Never run out of powdery trails at one of the largest ski resorts in the country.

Only spot in the U.S. where the borders of four states come together

BOREDOM BUSTER!
Keep an eye out for signs marking the Continental Divide, the line along the Rockies that separates rivers that flow into the Atlantic Ocean and rivers that flow into the Pacific Ocean.

INDEPENDENCE PASS
Elevation 12,095 feet
CONTINENTAL DIVIDE

5 COOL THINGS TO DO HERE

2 PIKES PEAK
Near Colorado Springs

Drive to the 14,115-foot (4,302-m) summit of one of the country's most visited mountains and take in the view that inspired "America the Beautiful."

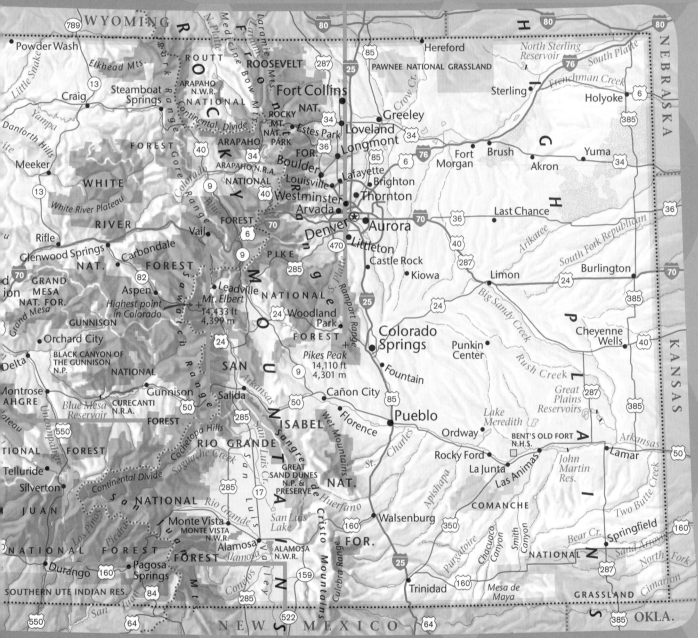

4 CLIFF PALACE
Mesa Verde National Park

Explore the largest cliff dwelling in America (150 rooms!)—and wonder why its ancestral Puebloan builders abandoned it 700 years ago.

5 RAILROAD TOUR
Durango

Climb aboard an 1882 locomotive and ride the rails through the San Juan Mountains to the mining town of Silverton.

5 COOL THINGS TO DO HERE

1 WOODEN ROLLER COASTER
Bristol

Shake, rattle, and roar down the track of Boulder Dash at Lake Compounce, North America's oldest amusement park.

2 TOROSAURUS
New Haven

Dinosaurs died out 65 million years ago, but their sculptures and fossilized skeletons still rule at Yale University's Peabody Museum of Natural History.

3 HARBOR SEALS
Thimble Islands

Board a boat and watch migrating seals waddle ashore on these stony islands once raided by the pirate Captain Kidd.

4 U.S.S. NAUTILUS
Groton

Explore the control room, crew quarters, and torpedo chamber of the world's first nuclear-powered submarine.

STATE CAPITAL: Hartford
AREA: 5,543 sq mi (14,357 sq km)

STATE BIRD: American robin

STATE FLOWER: mountain laurel

STATE ANIMAL: sperm whale

CONNECTICUT

The Constitution STATE

5 MYSTIC SEAPORT
Mystic

Finding this restored 18th-century whaling village is easy—just look for the towering masts of its old schooners and square-rigged ships.

Tour this southwestern corner of New England, and you'll soon see why so many people come here for a break from the bustle of nearby cities. Connecticut is a land of scenic seascapes, lush landscapes, and laid-back adventures.

BICYCLES
65
SPEED LIMIT

TRAFFIC LAWS YOU WON'T BELIEVE

Police can pull you over if you ride your bicycle faster than 65 miles an hour (105 km/h).

In Hartford, it's illegal to cross a street while walking on your hands.

It's illegal to drive a lawn mower faster than four miles an hour (6 km/h).

GPS BOREDOM BUSTER!
For such a small state, Connecticut sure has a lot of lakes—more than a thousand! How many can you find with your GPS?

Roadside Attractions

FROG BRIDGE
Gigantic bronze frogs crouch atop oversize thread spools on this unusual bridge in Willimantic.

FANCY SODAS
Make your own special soda at Avery's Beverages bottling plant in New Britain. Tour the factory and check out the mixing room, too.

MARK TWAIN HOUSE
Some claim this Hartford home of the famous author was built to resemble a Mississippi steamboat. Learn the truth when you take the tour.

STATE BIRD: blue hen chicken

STATE FLOWER: peach blossom

STATE ANIMAL: gray fox

STATE CAPITAL: Dover
AREA: 2,489 sq mi (6,447 sq km)

DELAWARE
The First STATE

#1 #1 #1 #1

Roadside Attractions

Delaware is a small state best known for big business, but that doesn't mean fun and games aren't on the agenda! Miles of Atlantic Ocean beaches beckon surfers and fishermen. Inland, you'll find massive mansions, fun museums, and the historic landmarks of the first colony to become a U.S. state.

TRAFFIC LAWS
YOU WON'T BELIEVE

Take Fido for a walk in South Bethany without using a doggy-doo bag and you risk paying a $100 fine!

You can't cook inside your car on Fenwick Island.

If Halloween falls on a Sunday, kids in Rehoboth Beach have to trick or treat the night before.

MILES THE MONSTER
Beware of the 50-foot (15-m) concrete creature clutching a race car at the Dover International Speedway.

GIANT STETHOSCOPE
This oversize medical tool hangs from a steel sculpture of a doctor's bag in front of a Newark hospital. At least Miles the Monster knows where to go for a checkup!

MYSTERIOUS MERMAN
The Zwaanendael Museum in Lewes is home to an interesting piece of art: a half-monkey/half-fish monstrosity that was cobbled together in the 19th century as a sideshow oddity.

GPS BOREDOM BUSTER!
A portion of Delaware's border is called the "Twelve-Mile Circle." Use your GPS to find this unusual feature and guess how it got its name.

24

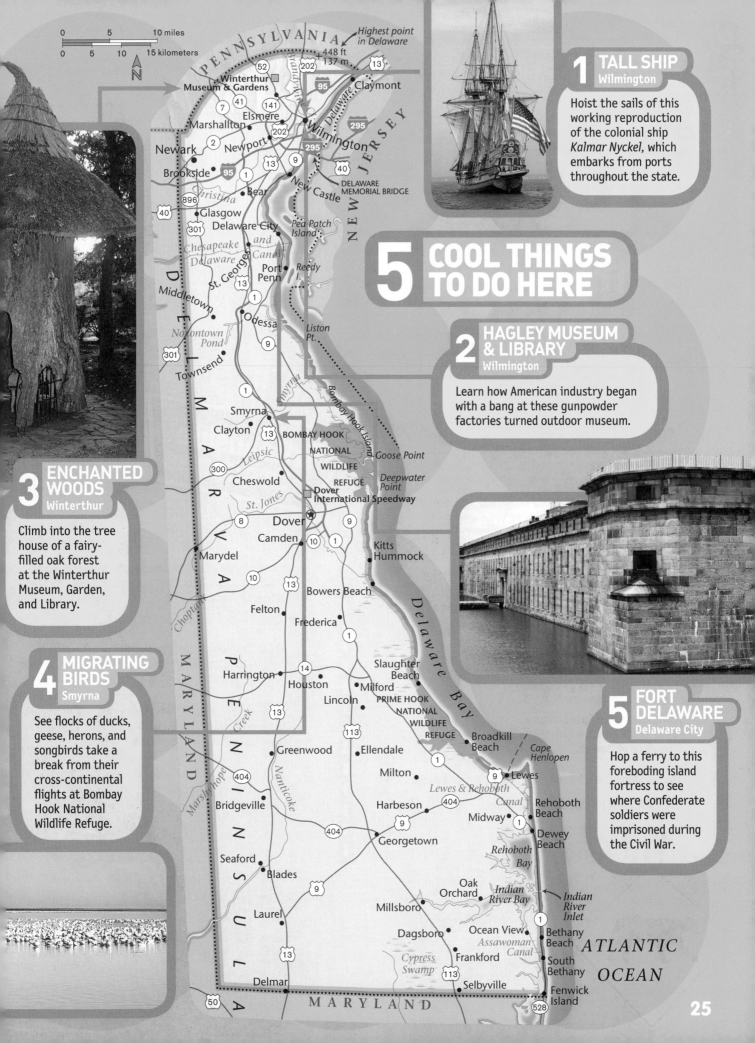

Highest point in Delaware
448 ft
137 m

1 TALL SHIP
Wilmington

Hoist the sails of this working reproduction of the colonial ship *Kalmar Nyckel*, which embarks from ports throughout the state.

5 COOL THINGS TO DO HERE

2 HAGLEY MUSEUM & LIBRARY
Wilmington

Learn how American industry began with a bang at these gunpowder factories turned outdoor museum.

3 ENCHANTED WOODS
Winterthur

Climb into the tree house of a fairy-filled oak forest at the Winterthur Museum, Garden, and Library.

4 MIGRATING BIRDS
Smyrna

See flocks of ducks, geese, herons, and songbirds take a break from their cross-continental flights at Bombay Hook National Wildlife Refuge.

5 FORT DELAWARE
Delaware City

Hop a ferry to this foreboding island fortress to see where Confederate soldiers were imprisoned during the Civil War.

Map labels:

PENNSYLVANIA
MARYLAND
NEW JERSEY
DELAWARE
DELMARVA PENINSULA
ATLANTIC OCEAN
Delaware Bay
Chesapeake and Delaware Canal

0 5 10 miles
0 5 10 15 kilometers

Winterthur Museum & Gardens
Claymont
Marshallton
Elsmere
Newport
Wilmington
Newark
Brookside
Bear
New Castle
DELAWARE MEMORIAL BRIDGE
Glasgow
Christina
Delaware City
St. Georges
Port Penn
Pea Patch Island
Reedy I.
Middletown
Odessa
Noxontown Pond
Liston Pt.
Townsend
Smyrna
Bombay Hook Island
Clayton
BOMBAY HOOK NATIONAL WILDLIFE REFUGE
Goose Point
Leipsic
Cheswold
Deepwater Point
St. Jones
Dover International Speedway
Dover
Camden
Kitts Hummock
Marydel
Bowers Beach
Felton
Frederica
Harrington
Houston
Slaughter Beach
Milford
Lincoln
PRIME HOOK NATIONAL WILDLIFE REFUGE
Greenwood
Ellendale
Milton
Broadkill Beach
Cape Henlopen
Lewes
Lewes & Rehoboth Canal
Bridgeville
Harbeson
Midway
Rehoboth Beach
Dewey Beach
Seaford
Blades
Georgetown
Rehoboth Bay
Oak Orchard
Indian River Bay
Indian River Inlet
Laurel
Millsboro
Dagsboro
Ocean View
Assawoman Canal
Bethany Beach
Frankford
South Bethany
Cypress Swamp
Selbyville
Fenwick Island
Delmar
Choptank
Marshyhope Creek
Nanticoke

25

STATE BIRD: mockingbird

STATE FLOWER: orange blossom

STATE ANIMAL: panther

STATE CAPITAL: Tallahassee
AREA: 65,755 sq mi (170,304 sq km)

Highest point in Florida
Britton I
345 ft 105
Crestview
Perdido
29
Pensacola
98
Fo
W
Be
GULF ISLANDS
NAT. SEASHOR

0 25 50 75 m
0 25 50 75 100 kilome

N

FLORIDA
The Sunshine STATE

S panish conquistador Ponce de León never found the Fountain of Youth when he explored Florida 500 years ago, yet the Sunshine State—land of Mickey Mouse, unending beaches, and vibrant cities— still brings out the kid in its many visitors.

FANTASTIC FLORIDA FACTS

Florida's original Spanish name is La Florida, which means "the place of flowers."

The Sunshine State has 663 miles (1,067 km) of beaches.

Orange juice is Florida's state beverage.

Roadside Attractions

WHIMZEYLAND
You'll do a double take when you drive by the wacky bowling ball sculptures in front of this colorful home in Safety Harbor.

GOOFY GOLF
A popular stop since 1959, this Putt-Putt course in Panama City features monsters, a volcano, and more!

SUNKEN GARDENS
What started as a St. Petersburg sinkhole 100 years ago is now a lush garden with waterfalls, exotic plants, and flocks of flamingos.

BOREDOM BUSTER!
Take a picture of every wacky road sign you pass and see how many you can find!

5 COOL THINGS TO DO HERE

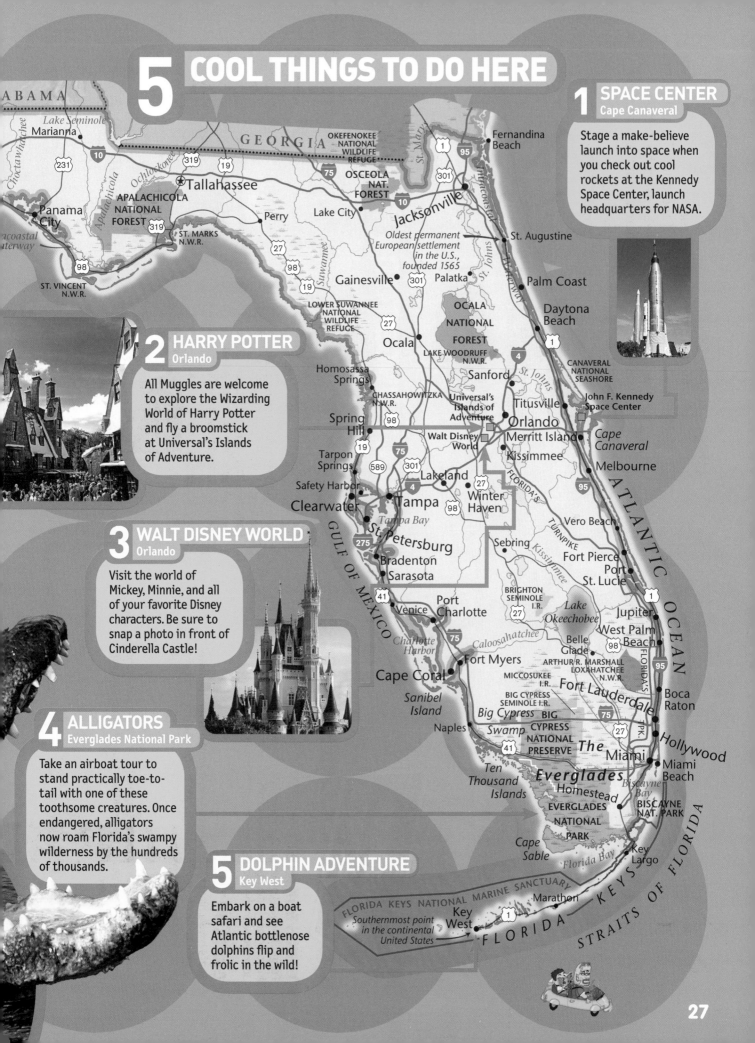

1 SPACE CENTER
Cape Canaveral

Stage a make-believe launch into space when you check out cool rockets at the Kennedy Space Center, launch headquarters for NASA.

2 HARRY POTTER
Orlando

All Muggles are welcome to explore the Wizarding World of Harry Potter and fly a broomstick at Universal's Islands of Adventure.

3 WALT DISNEY WORLD
Orlando

Visit the world of Mickey, Minnie, and all of your favorite Disney characters. Be sure to snap a photo in front of Cinderella Castle!

4 ALLIGATORS
Everglades National Park

Take an airboat tour to stand practically toe-to-tail with one of these toothsome creatures. Once endangered, alligators now roam Florida's swampy wilderness by the hundreds of thousands.

5 DOLPHIN ADVENTURE
Key West

Embark on a boat safari and see Atlantic bottlenose dolphins flip and frolic in the wild!

27

GEORGIA
The Peach STATE

STATE BIRD: brown thrasher

STATE CAPITAL: Atlanta
AREA: 59,425 sq mi (153,910 sq km)

STATE FLOWER: Cherokee rose

STATE TREE: live oak

G eorgia is full of must-see destinations, from energetic Atlanta to laid-back barrier islands. It's called the Peach State because it grows lots of these juicy fruits. Georgia is also home to the Okefenokee Swamp, the largest swamp in North America, where visitors can enjoy the great outdoors. You may even spot an alligator!

FANTASTIC GEORGIA FACTS

Chickens can't cross public roads in Athens-Clarke County.

Goldfish can't be given away as prizes in Athens-Clarke County.

Slingshots are outlawed on the streets of Columbus.

Roadside Attractions

LUNCH BOX MUSEUM
Forget the bag you use to haul your PB&J today. This museum in Columbus is devoted entirely to old-school metal lunch boxes adorned with the images of TV characters and superheroes.

GOATS ON THE ROOF
Goats have a blast hanging out on the roof of this fun roadside stop in Tiger. Give them a wave as you try gem mining and have some homemade ice cream.

OLD CAR CITY
Check out more than 4,000 classic American cars, trucks, vans, and a few school buses at the world's largest known classic car junkyard in the town of White.

5 COOL THINGS TO DO HERE

1 AMICALOLA FALLS
Amicalola Falls State Park

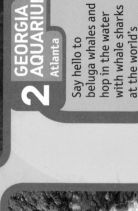

Climb steep stairways alongside this tumbling torrent in the Blue Ridge Mountains, not far from the start of the famous Appalachian Trail. At 729 feet (222 m), it is the tallest waterfall in Georgia.

2 GEORGIA AQUARIUM
Atlanta

Say hello to beluga whales and hop in the water with whale sharks at the world's largest aquarium.

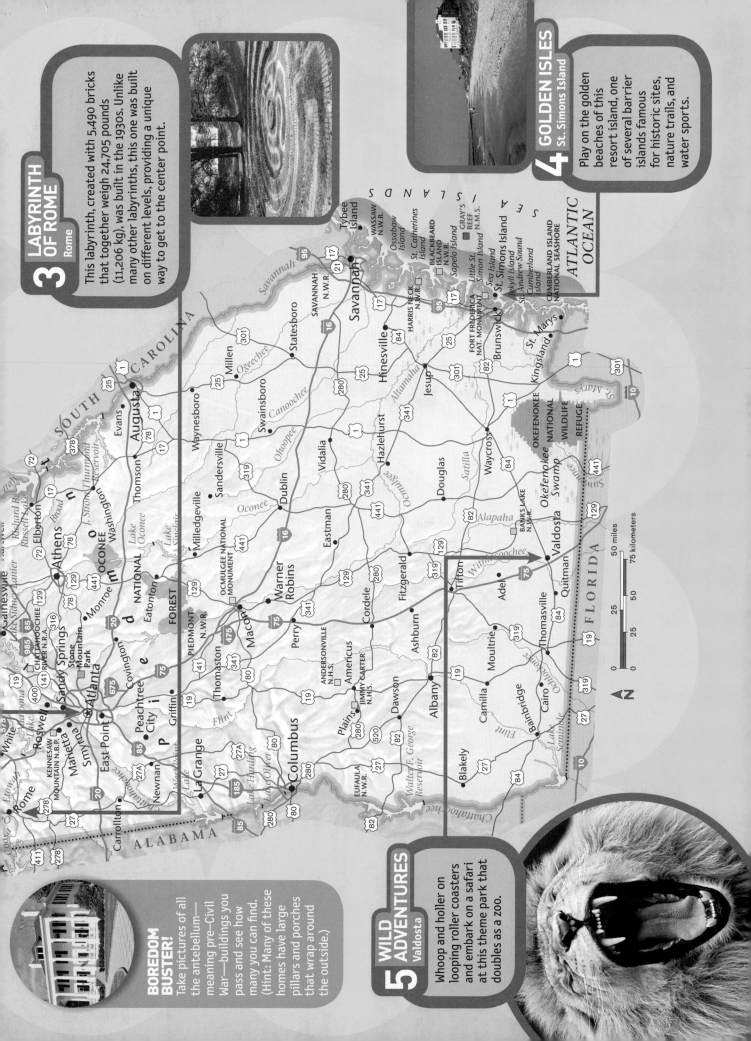

3 LABYRINTH OF ROME
Rome

This labyrinth, created with 5,490 bricks that together weigh 24,705 pounds (11,206 kg), was built in the 1930s. Unlike many other labyrinths, this one was built on different levels, providing a unique way to get to the center point.

4 GOLDEN ISLES
St. Simons Island

Play on the golden beaches of this resort island, one of several barrier islands famous for historic sites, nature trails, and water sports.

BOREDOM BUSTER!

Take pictures of all the antebellum—meaning pre–Civil War—buildings you pass and see how many you can find. (Hint: Many of these homes have large pillars and porches that wrap around the outside.)

5 WILD ADVENTURES
Valdosta

Whoop and holler on looping roller coasters and embark on a safari at this theme park that doubles as a zoo.

| **STATE BIRD:** Hawaiian goose | **STATE FLOWER:** hibiscus | |
| **STATE CAPITAL:** Honolulu AREA: 10,931 sq mi (28,311 sq km) | **STATE ANIMAL:** monk seal | |

HAWAII

The Aloha STATE

KAUA'I

Princeville · 560 · 56

Wai'ale'ale 5,148 ft 1,569 m · Kapa'a

550 · Waimea Canyon · Hanamā'ulu

Lehua I. · Kekaha · 50 · Līhu'e

Pu'uwai · Kalāheo · 50

NI'IHAU · Kaulakahi Channel · Kaua'i Chan

0   20   40 miles
0   20   40   60 kilometers

Roadside Attractions

Thrust into the middle of the Pacific Ocean by volcanic eruption long ago, the Hawaiian Islands are a tropical paradise of lush jungles, awesome waterfalls, and turquoise waters. Millions of tourists flock each year to the newest U.S. state to frolic on golden beaches and experience Polynesian culture.

FANTASTIC HAWAII FACTS

The Hawaiian Islands are actually the tips of an immense underwater mountain range.

"Aloha" is a multipurpose Hawaiian word. Use it to say hello, goodbye, or to express affection.

Hawaiian sand comes in a rainbow of colors: black, red—even green!

ALOHA ELVIS STATUE
This bronze statue in Honolulu catches the king of rock-and-roll in mid-croon, just as he appeared in a concert here in 1973.

HALONA BLOWHOLE
Fed by an ancient lava tube, this seaside rock formation on Oahu blasts seawater 30 feet (9 m) high.

HOOLEHUA POST OFFICE
At this unique post office on Molokai, you can decorate and mail out your own coconut. The post office, started in 1991, mails about 3,000 coconuts a year!

BOREDOM BUSTER!
Use your camera to take action shots of surfers riding waves. Award yourself bonus points if you catch any surfers hanging ten (riding with every toe over the board's nose).

5 COOL THINGS TO DO HERE

1 HELICOPTER TOUR
Waimea Canyon

Soar above the waterfalls and rugged cliffs of Kauai's "Grand Canyon of the Pacific."

2 SNORKEL ADVENTURE
Molokini Island

Dive headfirst into an undersea world teeming with tropical fish, sea turtles, and many other amazing marine creatures.

3 HUMPBACK WHALES
Lahaina

Watch 40-ton (36-t) leviathans create incredible splashes off the west coast of Maui.

4 SURFING
Honolulu

Learn what Hawaiians call the "sport of kings" in the land where it was invented. The easy rollers on Oahu's Waikiki Beach are best for surfers-in-training.

5 KILAUEA VOLCANO
Hawaii Volcanoes National Park

Watch the Big Island of Hawaii grow inch by inch as molten lava spews into the sea to form new land.

Map labels

O'AHU
Kahuku Pt.
Waialua
La'ie
930
99
Hau'ula
83
83
Mililani Town
H2
Pearl City
Kāne'ohe
93
750
H3
Kailua
Waipahu
H1
76
Honolulu
H1
72
Pearl Harbor
Waikīkī Beach

Kaiwi Channel

MOLOKA'I
Kalaupapa
KALAUPAPA N.H.P.
Hālawa
Kualapu'u
460
470
Waialua
Hālena
450
Honokahua
Kaunakakai
Keomuku
30
340
Kahului
MAUI
Lāna'i City
440
Lahaina
Wailuku
311
36
Makawao
Kīhei
31
Pukalani
360
Kaumalapau
Mākena
37
377
Hāna
LĀNA'I
Kaupō
HALEAKALĀ N.P.

HAWAIIAN ISLANDS HUMPBACK WHALE NATIONAL MARINE SANCTUARY

KAHO'OLAWE
Molokini Island
'Alenuihāhā Channel

PACIFIC OCEAN

'Upolu Pt.
Kapa'au
270
250
240
Kukuihaele
Highest point in Hawai'i
PU'UKOHOLĀ HEIAU N.H.S.
19
Waimea (Kamuela)
HAWAI'I
Waikoloa
Mauna Kea
13,796 ft
4,205 m
19
HAKALAU FOREST N.W.R.
19
190
200
Hilo
Keāhole Pt.
Kalaoa
Kailua-Kona
200
11
KALOKO-HONOKŌHAU N.H.P.
Cape Kumukahi
Hōlualoa
Mauna Loa Observatory
Mountain View
11
Mauna Loa
13,679 ft
4,169 m
'Opihikao
Captain Cook
HAWAI'I
Kīlauea Caldera
PU'UHONUA O HŌNAUNAU N.H.P.
VOLCANOES
NATIONAL PARK
Pāhala
Kahuku
11
Kalae (South Point)
Southernmost point in the U.S.

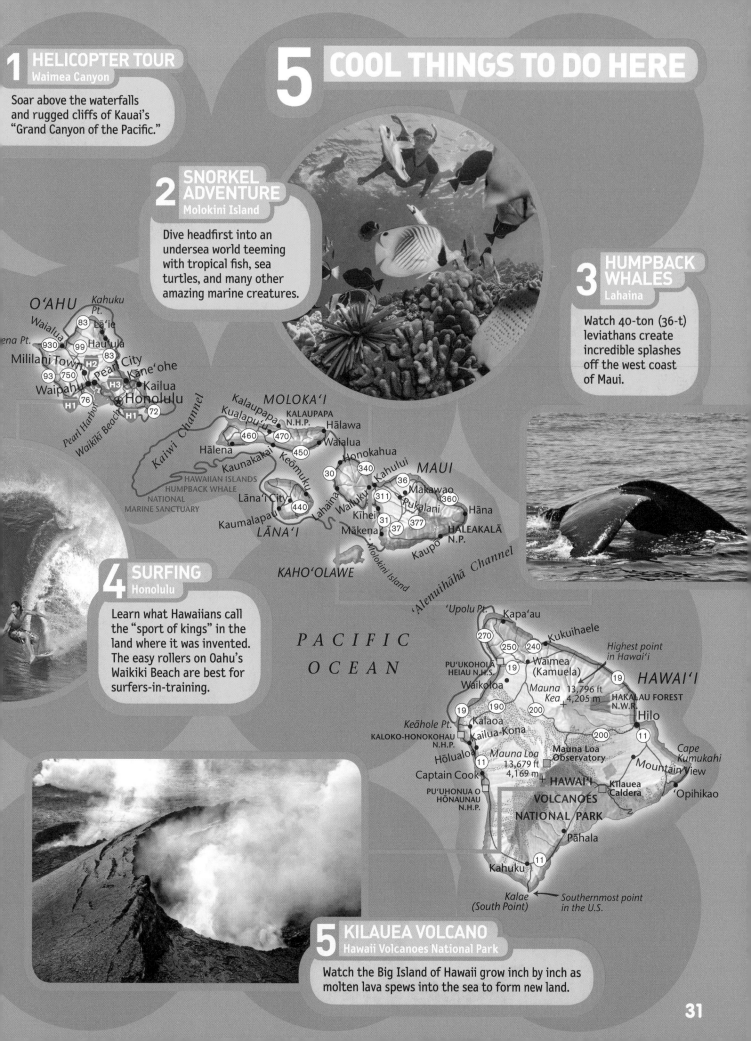

31

IDAHO
The Gem STATE

STATE BIRD: mountain bluebird

STATE FLOWER: syringa

STATE TREE: western white pine

STATE CAPITAL: Boise
AREA: 83,570 sq mi (216,447 sq km)

his state, perhaps best known for its spectacular spuds, offers unique and expansive landscapes such as Hells Canyon and Craters of the Moon. It got its nickname for its many scenic areas and for the many natural resources found here, including silver, copper, and gold.

Roadside Attractions

→ **IDAHO POTATO MUSEUM**
No spud detail is spared at this building in Blackfoot devoted to the history and deep-fried uses of Idaho's most famous crop.

→ **CITY OF ROCKS**
Stone formations in this Almo reserve almost look human-made. See rocks in the shapes of cities, castles, and animals—all the products of natural erosion.

→ **SHOSHONE ICE CAVES**
Residents from nearby Shoshone once chipped ice chunks from this frigid lava-made tube to keep their drinks cold. Now the caves make a refreshing roadside escape from Idaho's sweltering summer heat.

WHAT A SILLY SIGN!

What really happened to the chicken that crossed the road? This Caldwell street sign's nod to nuggets might finally solve the mystery.

CHICKEN DINNER RD
HWY 55

5 COOL THINGS TO DO HERE

1 HELLS CANYON
Hells Canyon National Recreation Area
Take a wild boat cruise between canyon walls that tower a mile (1.6 km) high in North America's deepest river gorge.

2 MOUNTAIN LAKES
Sawtooth National Recreation Area
Camp alongside pristine lakes that reflect the jutting peaks of the Sawtooths, one of the Rockies' many ranges.

5 CRATERS OF THE MOON
Craters of the Moon National Monument

Stroll through this jagged lunar-like landscape formed thousands of years ago when molten lava bubbled to Earth's surface.

3 BIRDS OF PREY
Morley Nelson Snake River Birds of Prey National Conservation Area

Watch bald eagles, peregrine falcons, and other regal raptors soar above this high-desert haven for nesting birds of prey.

4 SHOSHONE FALLS
Near Twin Falls

See the Snake River plunge 212 feet (64.6 m) over a series of craggy cliffs at this spectacular "Niagara of the West."

GPS BOREDOM BUSTER!

Use your GPS to hunt for any east-west routes crossing the state. Central Idaho's maze of Rocky Mountain peaks and rivers has defied travelers since the days of Lewis and Clark.

ILLINOIS
The Land of LINCOLN

This midwestern state is home to the Lake Michigan metropolis of Chicago and many don't-miss attractions. By contrast, vast agricultural lands around the state provide a fun balance to the big city's bustle. Illinois is home to more than 70,000 farms and produces more pumpkins than any other state!

STATE BIRD: cardinal

STATE FLOWER: violet

STATE ANIMAL: white-tailed deer

STATE CAPITAL: Springfield
AREA: 57,914 sq mi (149,998 sq km)

5 COOL THINGS TO DO HERE

1 WRIGLEY FIELD
Chicago

You don't need to be a Chicago Cubs fan to have a ball at this ivy-blanketed ballpark. The tasty Chicago-style hot dogs alone are worth the visit!

2 MUSEUM CAMPUS
Chicago

This park on the shores of Lake Michigan is home to a triple whammy of world-class museums: the Adler Planetarium, the Shedd Aquarium, and the fossil-filled Field Museum.

TRAFFIC LAWS
YOU WON'T BELIEVE

In Park Ridge, commercial trucks are not allowed to park in open parking lots without a permit.

In Cicero, musicians are not allowed to be seated when performing at restaurants.

You'd better ride your bicycle by the book in Galesburg, where fancy tricks are prohibited.

Roadside Attractions

METROPOLIS
This tiny town with a big name in southern Illinois is the official home of Superman. Fans will find a museum devoted to DC Comics' Man of Steel, among other super-duper tributes.

WORLD'S LARGEST CATSUP BOTTLE
If only this 170-foot (51.8-m) water tower in Collinsville were across the street from the world's largest plate of french fries ...

TWO-STORY OUTHOUSE
This wonder of outdoor plumbing makes for an unusual photo op—and rest stop—in the town of Gays.

LAKE MICHIGAN

WISCONSIN

Fox

Waukegan

Evanston
Park Ridge

Arlington Heights

Schaumburg

Cicero

Chicago

Belvidere

Elgin

Harvard

Rock

Pecatonica

Rockford

Sycamore

DeKalb

Naperville

Aurora

Sandwich

Freeport

Grand Detour

Savanna

Dixon

Sterling

Charles
Mound
1,235
ft 376 m

Highest point
in Illinois

Galena

UPPER

MISSISSIPPI

MISSISSIPPI RIVER

NATIONAL
WILDLIFE
AND FISH
REFUGE

Tampico

Mendota

Green
Rock

Moline

Hennepin

Joliet

94

45

41

294

12

355

34

30

39

88

90

120

47

14

43

Fox

20

80

280

80

80

55

90

3 COOL CANYONS
Starved Rock State Park

About 100 miles (161 km) from the skyscrapers of Chicago are skyscrapers of another kind: Starved Rock's geological wonderland of waterfalls and sandstone cliffs.

4 MILLER PARK ZOO
Bloomington

Visit red pandas, river otters, and bald eagles at this zoo filled with wildlife of land, water, and air.

GPS BOREDOM BUSTER!

Use your GPS to search for all the historic sites tied to Abraham Lincoln, who practiced law in central Illinois before becoming president.

5 ANCIENT CITY
Cahokia Mounds State Historic Site

Investigate the mysterious prehistoric culture of Cahokia, a mound city that rivaled medieval London in size, centuries before Columbus reached America.

STATE BIRD: cardinal

STATE FLOWER: peony

STATE TREE: tulip tree

STATE CAPITAL: Indianapolis
AREA: 36,418 sq mi (94,322 sq km)

INDIANA
The Hoosier STATE

C alled the "crossroads of America" for its spiderweb of roadways that connect the Midwest, Indiana is home to sandy beaches, fun museums, and Amish villages. Stop the car and see for yourself!

FANTASTIC INDIANA FACTS

The Indy 500 has been held at a racetrack in the state capital nearly every year since 1911.

Indiana's state tree, the tulip tree, usually grows to be 100 feet (30 m) tall or more.

Abraham Lincoln lived in Indiana from age 7 until he was 21 years old.

Roadside Attractions

GIANT BASKETBALL SNEAKER

A truck-size athletic shoe stands in front of a sports-themed hotel in New Castle. Don't worry, no stinky socks here!

YODER POPCORN

Sample a yummy variety of perfectly popped kernels from corn grown right outside this old-fashioned shop in Topeka.

SANTA CLAUS

Every day is a holiday in Santa Claus, a real town full of Christmas-themed attractions.

5 COOL THINGS TO DO HERE

1 LAKE DUNES
Indiana Dunes National Park

Get a concentrated dose of nature—from beach dunes to soggy swamps—in this wildly diverse park on the shore of Lake Michigan.

MICHIGAN

LAKE MICHIGAN

East Chicago

Hammond

Gary

Michigan City

INDIANA DUNES NATIONAL PARK

Portage

Merrillville

Crown Point

Lowell

Valparaiso

LaPorte

South Bend

Mishawaka

Elkhart

Goshen

Nappanee

Warsaw

Shipshewana

Topeka

Angola

Auburn

Kendallville

Columbia City

Fort Wayne

Plymouth

4 RACE CARS
Indianapolis

Climb into the cockpit of a sleek race car at the Indianapolis Motor Speedway Hall of Fame Museum.

5 HEDGE LABYRINTH
New Harmony

Make your way through the confounding hedge labyrinth of this serene historic town.

BOREDOM BUSTER!
No one knows for sure why Indiana is called the Hoosier State. Use a smartphone to research the many theories and choose the most likely among them.

2 AMISH COUNTRY
Shipshewana

Tour the villages and sample the homemade treats of Indiana's Amish, a community that embraces 19th-century living for religious reasons.

3 CHILDREN'S MUSEUM
Indianapolis

Touching the exhibits is encouraged at this popular hands-on science museum.

Highest point in Indiana
1,257 ft 383 m +

80 miles
120 kilometers
0   40   80
0   40
N

KENTUCKY

HOOSIER NATIONAL FOREST

BROWN COUNTY STATE PARK

MUSCATATUCK N.W.R.

LINCOLN BOYHOOD NATIONAL MEMORIAL

GEORGE ROGERS CLARK N.H.P.

ILLINOIS

37

STATE BIRD: eastern goldfinch

STATE FLOWER: wild rose

STATE TREE: oak

STATE CAPITAL: Des Moines
AREA: 56,272 sq mi (145,743 sq km)

IOWA

The Hawkeye STATE

Rolling hills, big red barns, and endless stalks of corn rush past your window as you ride through Iowa. To see the state's most valuable resource, however, you'll need to pull over and get your hands dirty. Iowa's black soil is the most fertile in the country. The state's nickname is a tribute to Chief Black Hawk, who was leader of the Native American Sauk tribe.

TRAFFIC LAWS YOU WON'T BELIEVE

It's illegal to pick a flower in a city park in Mount Vernon.

You'll need permission from Mount Vernon's city council if you plan to toss bricks onto a highway.

You'll never hear the catchy tune of an ice-cream truck in Indianola, which banned the vehicles.

BOREDOM BUSTER!
Use a smartphone to look up all the famous people born in Iowa and see how many you can find!

Roadside Attractions

VERMEER WINDMILL
Take a peek at the gears and grain-grinding power of the country's tallest working windmill, towering above the Dutch-settled town of Pella.

BUFFALO BILL MUSEUM
Learn about one of the Wild West's most colorful cowboys in LeClaire, birthplace of William F. "Buffalo Bill" Cody.

AMERICAN GOTHIC HOUSE
Re-create the famous painting "American Gothic" by posing in front of the historic house in Eldon that inspired it.

Map labels: SOUTH DAKOTA, NEBRASKA, Missouri, Big Sioux, Floyd, Little Sioux, Hawkeye Poi 1,670 ft 509, Highest point in Iowa, Sioux Center, Orange City, Le Mars, Cher, Sioux City, Onawa, DE SOTO, Co Blu, Gle, 75, 90, 18, 29, 75, 20, 34, 680, 80

HINGS TO DO HERE

1 ADVENTURELAND
Altoona

Strap into any of the many roller coasters at this tons-of-fun amusement park.

2 MYSTERIOUS MOUNDS
Near Marquette

Native Americans built sacred mounds in the shape of birds and bears long ago. Explore the Effigy Mounds National Monument to find out why.

EFFIGY MOUNDS
NATIONAL MONUMENT
Headquarters-Visitor Center-Museum →

Map labels

MINNESOTA

WISCONSIN

ILLINOIS

MISSOURI

N

0   25   50 miles
0   25   50   75 kilometers

Lake
West Okoboji Lake
East Okoboji Lake
Estherville
UNION SLOUGH N.W.R.
Forest City
Emmetsburg
Clear Lake
Algona
Humboldt
Fort Dodge
Webster City
Mason City
Hampton
Iowa Falls
Eldora
Story City
Boone
Marshalltown
Ames
Nevada
Carroll
Jefferson
Perry
Ankeny
Urbandale
Des Moines
Windsor Heights
West Des Moines
Altoona
Newton
Grinnell
Winterset
Indianola
Pella
Knoxville
Osceola
Chariton
Oskaloosa
Ottumwa
Creston
Centerville
Bloomfield
Red Oak
Clarinda
Bedford
Blanchard

Cresco
Osage
Decorah
Waukon
New Hampton
Charles City
Waverly
Oelwein
EFFIGY MOUNDS N.M.
Marquette
Dubuque
Waterloo
Cedar Falls
Independence
Manchester
Dyersville
Monticello
Central City
Vinton
Marion
Anamosa
Maquoketa
Cedar Rapids
Mount Vernon
De Witt
Clinton
SAC AND FOX/ MESKWAKI INDIAN RES.
HERBERT HOOVER N.H.S.
Coralville
Iowa City
Bettendorf
Davenport
Le Claire
Muscatine
Washington
MARK TWAIN N.W.R.
Fairfield
Burlington
Eldon
Mount Pleasant
Fort Madison
Keokuk

NEAL SMITH N.W.R.
Lake Red Rock
Rathbun Lake

NATIONAL WILDLIFE & FISH REFUGE

Des Moines River
Raccoon
Boone
Iowa
Cedar
Shell Rock
Winnebago
Wapsipinicon
Upper Iowa
Turkey
Maquoketa
Mississippi River
Thompson
E. Nodaway
Chariton
Des Moines

UPPER MISSISSIPPI RIVER

3 HOT-AIR BALLOONS
Indianola

Hot-air flight makes history at the National Balloon Museum, where you can also hop aboard a basket for an adventure in the skies with a local tour group.

4 LIVING HISTORY FARMS
Urbandale

Take a fascinating look at where your food comes from by exploring three historic farms, including one run by Native Americans.

5 FOSSILS
Coralville

A 1993 flood scoured away trees and soil at the Devonian Fossil Gorge, revealing the petrified skeletons of sea creatures that died 150 million years before the age of dinosaurs.

STATE FLOWER: sunflower

STATE ANIMAL: buffalo

STATE CAPITAL: Topeka
AREA: 82,277 sq mi (213,097 sq km)

KANSAS

The Sunflower STATE

Roadside Attractions

That hint of earthy flavor in your bread? That's Kansas you're tasting! Most of America's wheat grows here in the nation's geographic heart. What else makes Kansas special? Fields of glorious sunflowers, which reach peak bloom in September, can be seen across the state.

TRAFFIC LAWS YOU WON'T BELIEVE

It's illegal to ride a zebra down the road in Derby.

Better pull over if you see a marching band coming your way in Topeka, where driving through parades is not allowed.

Using a musical instrument on Topeka's streets for the purpose of attracting attention is a big no-no.

ROCK CITY
The sandstone boulders scattered around this park near Minneapolis aren't petrified dinosaur eggs. They're actually geological leftovers from when Kansas was covered by a vast inland sea.

DOROTHY'S HOUSE
How do you find the house that fell on the Wicked Witch of the East in *The Wizard of Oz*? Follow the yellow brick road in Liberal, of course.

MUSEUM OF WORLD TREASURES
T. rex fossils, ancient Egyptian mummies, and other artifacts fill three floors of time-tripping exhibits in Wichita.

STORM SHELTER

BOREDOM BUSTER!
Take a picture of every tornado shelter sign you pass and see how many you can find!

5 COOL THINGS TO DO HERE

1 MONUMENT ROCKS
Near Oakley

Explore an alien landscape of towering chalk formations in the vast prairie-land of northwestern Kansas.

2 TALLGRASS PRAIRIE
Flint Hills

Watch fireflies flit above this green-and-golden oasis, all that remains of a vast sea of grass that once covered 170 million acres (69 million ha) of North America.

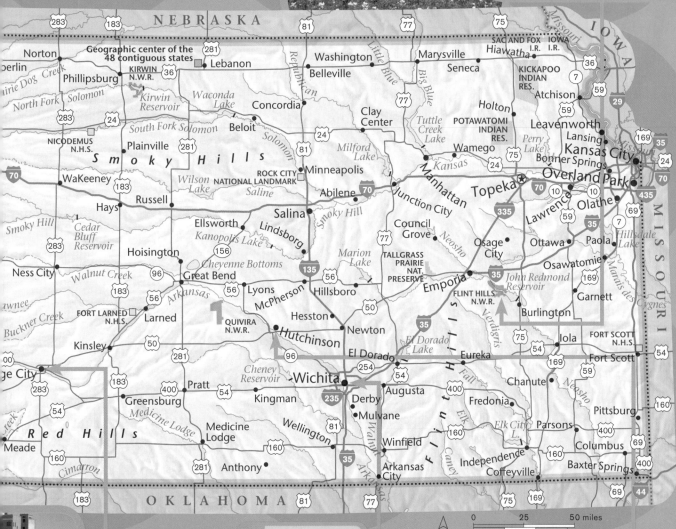

3 WILD WEST
Dodge City

The Boot Hill Museum on Front Street re-creates Dodge City during the lawless 1870s, when gun-slingers like Wyatt Earp enforced frontier justice.

4 SEDGWICK COUNTY ZOO
Wichita

Grizzly bears, bison, wolves, and other prairie creatures are in plain sight at this zoo's North American exhibits.

5 COSMOSPHERE
Hutchinson

You won't believe you're in Kansas anymore when you explore this shrine to the space race. Only Washington, D.C.'s Air and Space Museum has more out-of-this-world artifacts.

KENTUCKY

The Bluegrass STATE

Roadside Attractions

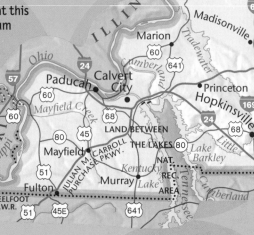

0   25   50 m
0   25   50   75 kilom

Kentucky is famous for two distinct sounds: the thunderous gallop of thoroughbred horses and the toe-tapping twang of bluegrass music. You're bound to hear one or the other as you ramble from the state's Appalachian highlands to its rolling farmland.

FANTASTIC KENTUCKY FACTS

Over 147 million ounces (almost 4.2 million kg) of gold are locked away in Fort Knox, the world's most secure vault.

Near Louisville, tour the birthplace and boyhood home of Abraham Lincoln, the first U.S. president born west of the Appalachian Mountains.

Eastern Kentucky is home to so many country music stars that a stretch of highway was renamed the "Country Music Highway."

GPS BOREDOM BUSTER!
Use your GPS to find a horse ranch near you—then snap a photo of a thoroughbred galloping through a roadside pasture!

THE BLUEGRASS MUSIC HALL OF FAME & MUSEUM
Listen and learn at this Owensboro museum dedicated to the music of Kentucky's bluegrass plains.

HARLAND SANDERS CAFÉ AND MUSEUM
Harland Sanders—aka Colonel Sanders to fast-food aficionados—opened his first restaurant in Corbin. Visit to see the birthplace of Kentucky Fried Chicken.

KENTUCKY CASTLE
Perched in the rolling pasturelands of Versailles, this themed hotel looks just like a medieval fortress. Well, aside from the swimming pool and tennis courts.

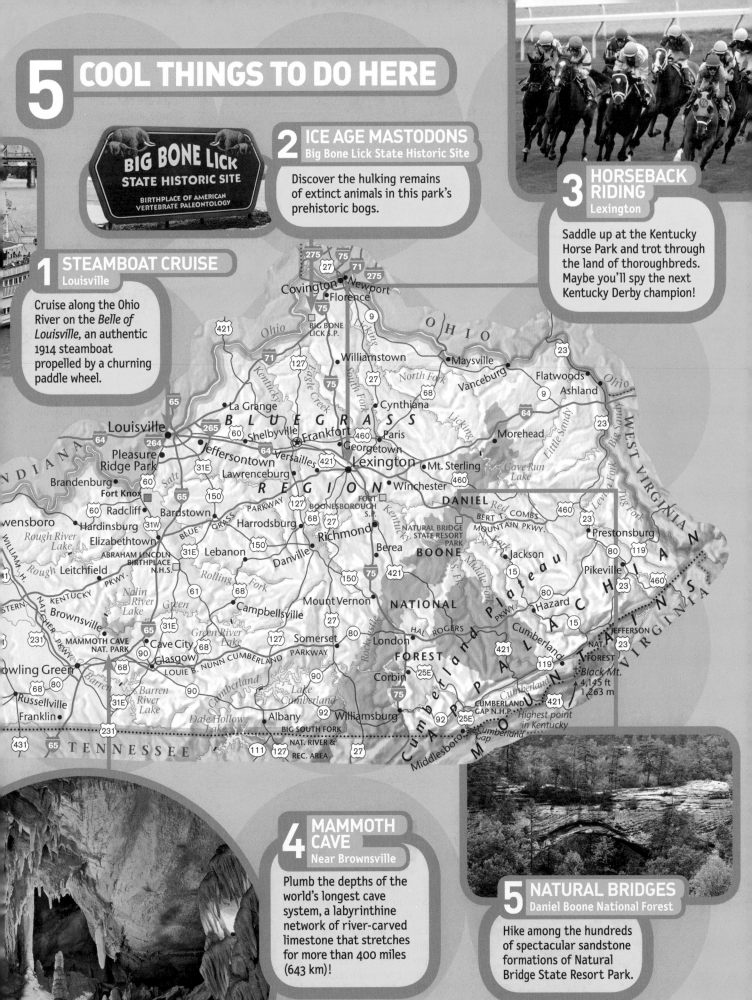

5 COOL THINGS TO DO HERE

BIG BONE LICK STATE HISTORIC SITE
BIRTHPLACE OF AMERICAN VERTEBRATE PALEONTOLOGY

2 ICE AGE MASTODONS
Big Bone Lick State Historic Site

Discover the hulking remains of extinct animals in this park's prehistoric bogs.

3 HORSEBACK RIDING
Lexington

Saddle up at the Kentucky Horse Park and trot through the land of thoroughbreds. Maybe you'll spy the next Kentucky Derby champion!

1 STEAMBOAT CRUISE
Louisville

Cruise along the Ohio River on the *Belle of Louisville*, an authentic 1914 steamboat propelled by a churning paddle wheel.

4 MAMMOTH CAVE
Near Brownsville

Plumb the depths of the world's longest cave system, a labyrinthine network of river-carved limestone that stretches for more than 400 miles (643 km)!

5 NATURAL BRIDGES
Daniel Boone National Forest

Hike among the hundreds of spectacular sandstone formations of Natural Bridge State Resort Park.

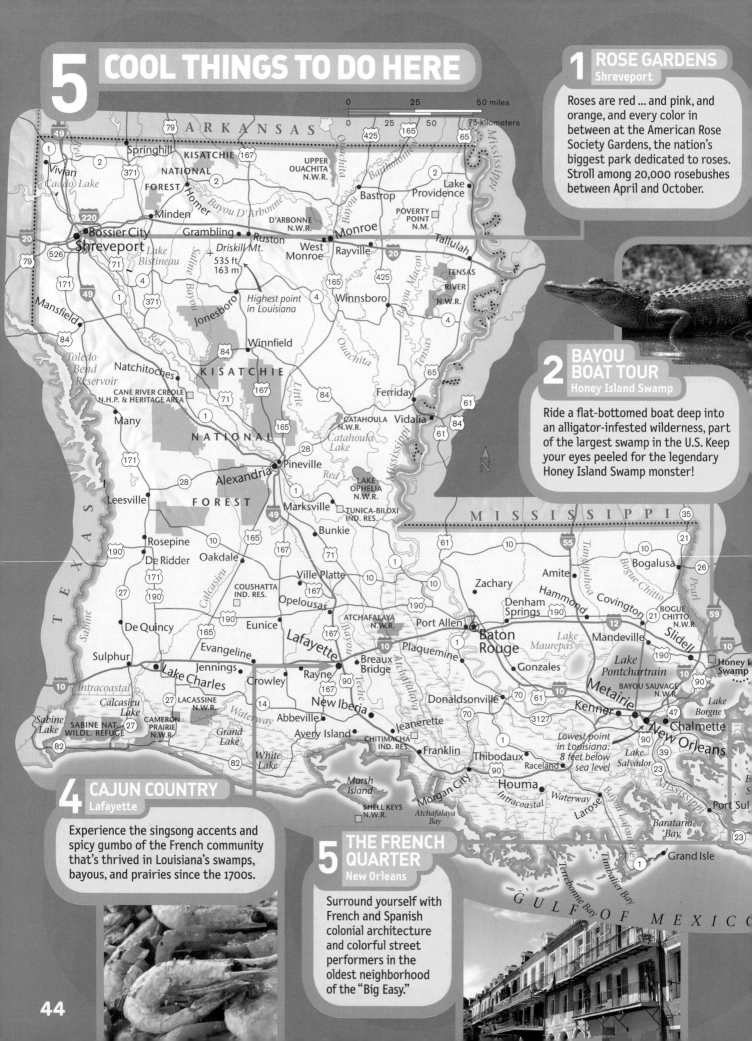

5 COOL THINGS TO DO HERE

Scale: 0 — 25 — 50 miles / 0 — 25 — 50 — 75 kilometers

1 ROSE GARDENS
Shreveport

Roses are red ... and pink, and orange, and every color in between at the American Rose Society Gardens, the nation's biggest park dedicated to roses. Stroll among 20,000 rosebushes between April and October.

2 BAYOU BOAT TOUR
Honey Island Swamp

Ride a flat-bottomed boat deep into an alligator-infested wilderness, part of the largest swamp in the U.S. Keep your eyes peeled for the legendary Honey Island Swamp monster!

4 CAJUN COUNTRY
Lafayette

Experience the singsong accents and spicy gumbo of the French community that's thrived in Louisiana's swamps, bayous, and prairies since the 1700s.

5 THE FRENCH QUARTER
New Orleans

Surround yourself with French and Spanish colonial architecture and colorful street performers in the oldest neighborhood of the "Big Easy."

Map labels

ARKANSAS

MISSISSIPPI

TEXAS

GULF OF MEXICO

Springhill, Vivian, Caddo Lake, Minden, Bossier City, Shreveport, Lake Bistineau, Mansfield, KISATCHIE NATIONAL FOREST, Homer, Grambling, Ruston, Bayou D'Arbonne, D'ARBONNE N.W.R., UPPER OUACHITA N.W.R., Bastrop, West Monroe, Monroe, Rayville, Lake Providence, POVERTY POINT N.M., Tallulah, Driskill Mt. 535 ft / 163 m, Highest point in Louisiana, Jonesboro, Winnfield, Winnsboro, TENSAS RIVER N.W.R., Natchitoches, Toledo Bend Reservoir, CANE RIVER CREOLE N.H.P. & HERITAGE AREA, Many, KISATCHIE, Ferriday, Vidalia, CATAHOULA N.W.R., Catahoula Lake, Pineville, Alexandria, NATIONAL FOREST, Leesville, Marksville, TUNICA-BILOXI IND. RES., LAKE OPHELIA N.W.R., Bunkie, Rosepine, De Ridder, Oakdale, COUSHATTA IND. RES., Ville Platte, Opelousas, Eunice, Lafayette, ATCHAFALAYA N.W.R., De Quincy, Sulphur, Jennings, Lake Charles, Crowley, Rayne, Breaux Bridge, New Iberia, LACASSINE N.W.R., CAMERON PRAIRIE N.W.R., Abbeville, Avery Island, CHITIMACHA IND. RES., Jeanerette, Franklin, Sabine Lake, SABINE NAT. WILDL. REFUGE, Calcasieu Lake, Grand Lake, White Lake, Marsh Island, SHELL KEYS N.W.R., Morgan City, Atchafalaya Bay, Zachary, Denham Springs, Hammond, Amite, Covington, Bogalusa, BOGUE CHITTO N.W.R., Mandeville, Slidell, Port Allen, Baton Rouge, Gonzales, Plaquemine, Donaldsonville, Lake Maurepas, Lake Pontchartrain, Metairie, Kenner, New Orleans, Chalmette, BAYOU SAUVAGE N.W.R., Honey Island Swamp, Lake Borgne, Thibodaux, Raceland, Houma, Larose, Lake Salvador, Lowest point in Louisiana: 8 feet below sea level, Barataria Bay, Terrebonne Bay, Timbalier Bay, Grand Isle, Port Sul, Mississippi, Red, Ouachita, Tensas, Little, Sabine, Intracoastal Waterway

LOUISIANA

The Pelican STATE

Infused with pirate lore, voodoo magic, and the sweet sounds of jazz, Louisiana boasts a blend of French, Spanish, and West African cultures. Its volcanic Cajun cuisine, sultry swamps, and surreal celebrations will take your senses on a roller-coaster ride.

Roadside Attractions

3 AUDUBON AQUARIUM OF THE AMERICAS
New Orleans

This famous aquarium's clear tunnels and titanic tanks let you get as close as possible to aquatic life without getting wet.

FANTASTIC LOUISIANA FACTS

It's illegal to have a pig farm within two miles (1.6 km) of an Army camp in Jefferson Parish.

Alligators must stay at least 200 yards (182.8 m) away from the Mardi Gras Parade route.

Planting a tree near New Orleans streets or highways is a crime.

GPS BOREDOM BUSTER!
Use your GPS to find all the locations named after Jean Lafitte, a 19th-century pirate who became a New Orleans folk hero.

THE BIEDENHARN MUSEUM & GARDENS
Take a stroll through the historic home and magical gardens of Joseph A. Biedenharn, the first bottler of Coca-Cola.

MARDI GRAS WORLD
Can't make the annual Mardi Gras party? Visit Blaine Kern's Mardi Gras World in New Orleans to see how the parade's magical floats get made.

AUDUBON BUTTERFLY GARDEN AND INSECTARIUM
This New Orleans museum is infested with insects, but don't call the exterminator! The butterflies, spiders, and swarms of bugs here are all part of the exhibits.

STATE BIRD: black-capped chickadee

STATE ANIMAL: moose

STATE FLOWER: white pine cone and tassel

STATE CAPITAL: Augusta
AREA: 35,385 sq mi (91,646 sq km)

MAINE
The Pine Tree STATE

Y ou're more likely to meet a moose than a fellow traveler when you delve into the untamed wilderness of Maine, New England's largest state. Most visitors stick to the craggy coastline, famous for its lighthouses and lobster shacks.

FANTASTIC MAINE FACTS

Maine is larger than all five other New England states combined!

About 80 percent of the country's lobster is caught here.

Maine has more moose per square mile than any other state.

Roadside Attractions

➤ WORLD'S LARGEST ROTATING GLOBE
Mapping corporation DeLorme decorated its headquarters in Yarmouth with the biggest map of all—a four-story globe that rotates just like our home planet.

➤ GIANT BOOTS
The 16-foot (5-m) rubber boots outside the L.L. Bean clothing store in Freeport look a little large for the average outdoor enthusiast. Fortunately, the store sells them in smaller sizes.

➤ DESERT OF MAINE
A desert in the middle of Maine's green landscape might seem suspiciously out of place, but the dunes near Freeport weren't trucked in to create a tourist attraction. The "sand" here is actually ancient glacial silt uncovered by overfarming.

5 COOL THINGS TO DO HERE

★ 1 BAXTER STATE PARK
Central Maine
Take a hike way, way, way off the beaten path in the heart of Maine's mountainous wilderness, free from roads but full of moose!

St. Francis
Allagash
St. John
Saint John
Frenchville
Fort Kent
Madawaska
Van Buren
Limestone
Long Lake
Square Lake
Eagle L.
Eagle Lake
2
1
161
11
1A

0   25   50 miles

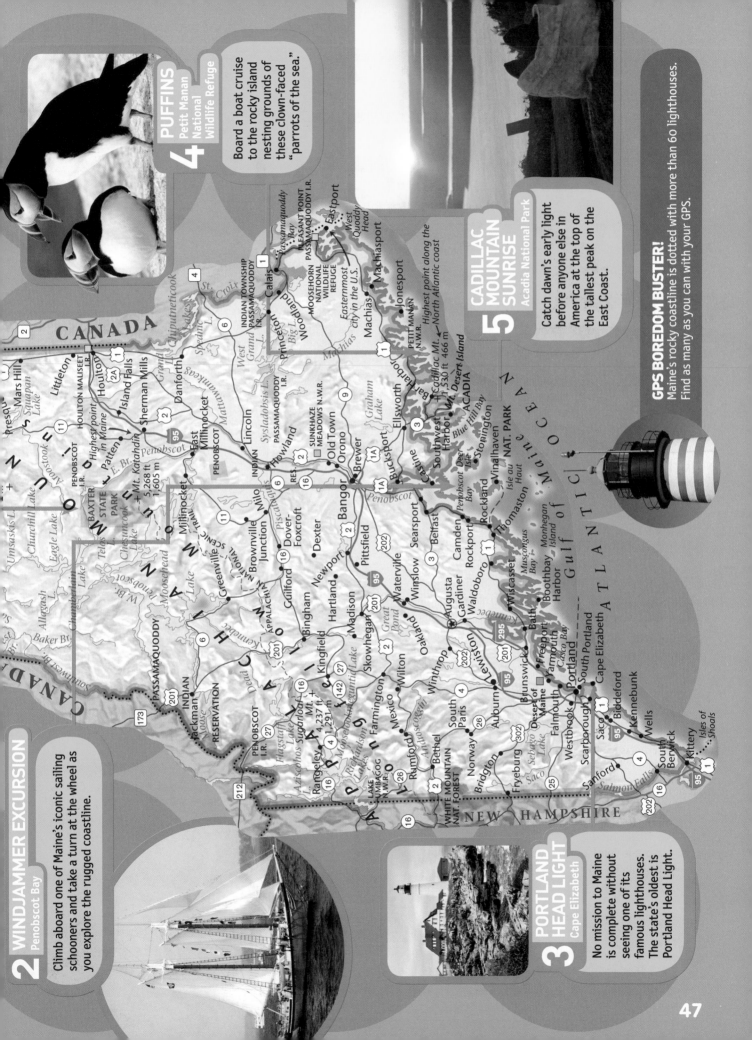

2 WINDJAMMER EXCURSION
Penobscot Bay

Climb aboard one of Maine's iconic sailing schooners and take a turn at the wheel as you explore the rugged coastline.

4 PUFFINS
Petit Manan National Wildlife Refuge

Board a boat cruise to the rocky island nesting grounds of these clown-faced "parrots of the sea."

5 CADILLAC MOUNTAIN SUNRISE
Acadia National Park

Catch dawn's early light before anyone else in America at the top of the tallest peak on the East Coast.

GPS BOREDOM BUSTER!
Maine's rocky coastline is dotted with more than 60 lighthouses. Find as many as you can with your GPS.

3 PORTLAND HEAD LIGHT
Cape Elizabeth

No mission to Maine is complete without seeing one of its famous lighthouses. The state's oldest is Portland Head Light.

47

 **STATE BIRD:** Baltimore oriole

 **STATE FLOWER:** black-eyed Susan

 STATE TREE: white oak

STATE CAPITAL: Annapolis
AREA: 12,407 sq mi (32,133 sq km)

MARYLAND

The Old Line STATE

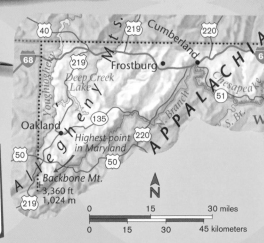

 **Roadside Attractions**

H ere's a tip to making the most of your trip to Maryland: Come in a crabby mood! This seaside state is famous for its blue crab, caught fresh from the Chesapeake Bay. Seafood not your style? Plenty of other nice— often nautical—attractions await.

FANTASTIC MARYLAND FACTS

Poet Francis Scott Key wrote the national anthem in 1814 after he watched the British Royal Navy bombard Fort McHenry.

Maryland gave up some of its land to help form the U.S. capital—Washington, D.C.

The average depth of Chesapeake Bay and its tributaries is only 21 feet (6.4 m).

GPS BOREDOM BUSTER!
Maryland is less than two miles (3.2 km) wide near the town of Hancock. Find this narrow patch with your GPS—then go walk across the state!

DINOSAUR PARK
Visit this cool park in Laurel where you can search for 115-million-year-old dinosaur fossils. Meet paleontologists and discover what Earth was like in the time of dinosaurs.

AMERICAN VISIONARY ART MUSEUM
This museum in Baltimore features the unique work of self-taught artists. A sculpture plaza and outdoor movie theater are all part of the fun!

B&O RAILROAD MUSEUM
Railroad history's mightiest locomotives fill this big Baltimore building—and spill into the parking lot.

5 COOL THINGS TO DO HERE

1 NATIONAL AQUARIUM
Baltimore

See dolphins, jellyfish, and some truly wild Australian reptiles at this aquarium in Baltimore's Inner Harbor.

2 MARYLAND SCIENCE CENTER
Baltimore

Pretend you're a paleontologist or an astronomer for a day at this museum that takes a hands-on approach to science.

3 TRIMPER'S RIDES
Ocean City

Ride old-fashioned merry-go-rounds and modern coasters at this century-old boardwalk amusement park.

4 CHESAPEAKE BAY CRUISE
Annapolis

No visit to "America's sailing capital" is complete without a day cruise along this inland coastline, or join a kayak tour and see historic Annapolis from a different perspective.

5 WILD HORSES
Assateague State Park

Some believe the wild horses that roam this small coastal island are descended from a herd of shipwreck survivors.

49

STATE BIRD: black-capped chickadee

STATE FLOWER: mayflower

STATE TREE: American elm

STATE CAPITAL: Boston
AREA: 10,555 sq mi (27,336 sq km)

MASSACHUSETTS

The Bay STATE

This New England state is rich in restful seaside villages and historic sites from every American era. Where did its nickname come from? Many of those seaside villages sit on several large and lovely bays that provide plenty of scenic harbors along the state's jutting coastline.

WHAT A SILLY SIGN!

Can funny signs save lives? Traffic officials in Massachusetts think so. They asked motorists to send in ideas for funny but informative electronic signs. Winners included "Use Yah Blinkah" and "Make Yah Ma Proud, War Yah Seatbelt."

Roadside Attractions

MAPPARIUM

Visitors to the Mary Baker Eddy Library in Boston get a new perspective on the world when they walk through the center of a three-story globe.

WHALING MUSEUM

The pursuit of whale oil and blubber was once big business in Massachusetts. This museum in New Bedford highlights the whaling trade's ships, tools, and dangers.

THE BUTTERFLY PLACE

Hundreds of butterflies flutter around this indoor garden in Westford.

3 OLD STURBRIDGE VILLAGE
Sturbridge

Experience ye olde New England at this 200-acre (81-ha) village staffed by historical interpreters who may convince you it's 1840.

BOREDOM BUSTER!

Both basketball and chocolate chip cookies have their origins in Massachusetts. Use a smartphone to look up other famous inventions from this New England state.

Salem Witch Museum 1692

5 COOL THINGS TO DO HERE

1 SALEM WITCH MUSEUM
Salem

Today's Harry Potter books have made heroes out of witches, but in 1692 witches were public enemy number one. Learn the tragic tale of Salem's witch trials at this scary museum.

2 FREEDOM TRAIL
Boston

Hike through history on this meandering path that visits the American Revolution's significant Boston landmarks, including Paul Revere's house and the site of the Boston Massacre.

4 MAYFLOWER II
Plymouth

Explore the shockingly cramped quarters of this stem-to-stern reproduction of the ship that carried 102 Pilgrims across the storm-tossed Atlantic Ocean in 1620.

5 FIN WHALES
Cape Cod

Board a boat bound for Stellwagen Bank National Marine Sanctuary to watch the world's second largest whales wave their flukes.

STATE BIRD: robin

STATE CAPITAL: Lansing
AREA: 96,716 sq mi (250,495 sq km)

STATE FLOWER: apple blossom

STATE ANIMAL: white-tailed deer

MICHIGAN
The Wolverine STATE

S urrounded by four of the Great Lakes, Michigan is almost an island state—two island states, actually! The mitten-shaped Lower Peninsula, home of the Detroit auto industry, is a high-octane world apart from the quiet wilderness of the Upper Peninsula.

▶ Roadside Attractions

MARVIN'S MARVELOUS MECHANICAL MUSEUM

The owner of this Farmington Hills arcade has amassed a collection of coin-operated oddities that seem positively prehistoric compared to today's video games.

FRANKENMUTH

A slice of traditional Germany is transplanted to this Lower Peninsula town famous for its yummy fudge and storybook decor.

WORLD'S LARGEST TIRE

The 80-foot (24-m) radial in Allen Park served as the hub of a Ferris wheel before it became a roadside curiosity.

WHAT A SILLY SIGN!

Perhaps it was temporary insanity that caused someone to name a private lane in Traverse City "Psycho Path."

5 COOL THINGS TO DO HERE

1 LAKE SUPERIOR CRUISE
Pictured Rocks National Lakeshore

The best way to take in the Upper Peninsula's rugged shoreline of cliffs and waterfalls is via a variety of boat tours, from kayaks to cruises, leaving from Munising.

2 MACKINAC ISLAND
Mackinac Island State Park

Step from the ferry onto this picturesque island and you'll notice something missing: cars! Bikes and horse-drawn carriages are the only ways to travel in this quaint island village.

CANADA

ISLE ROYALE NATIONAL PARK

Isle Royale

L A K E   S U P E R

Copper Harbor

KEWEENAW

41

Keweenaw

N

0   25   50   75 miles
0   25   50   75   100 kilometers

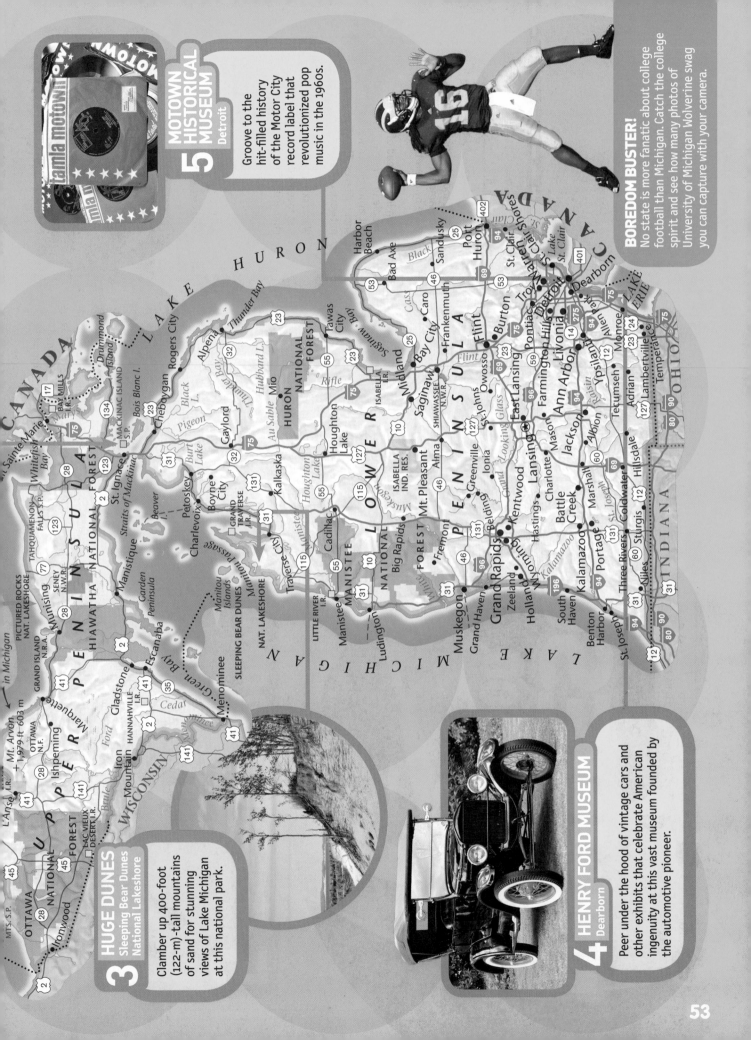

5 MOTOWN HISTORICAL MUSEUM
Detroit

Groove to the hit-filled history of the Motor City record label that revolutionized pop music in the 1960s.

BOREDOM BUSTER!
No state is more fanatic about college football than Michigan. Catch the college spirit and see how many photos of University of Michigan Wolverine swag you can capture with your camera.

3 HUGE DUNES
Sleeping Bear Dunes National Lakeshore

Clamber up 400-foot (122-m)-tall mountains of sand for stunning views of Lake Michigan at this national park.

4 HENRY FORD MUSEUM
Dearborn

Peer under the hood of vintage cars and other exhibits that celebrate American ingenuity at this vast museum founded by the automotive pioneer.

MINNESOTA

The Land of 10,000 LAKES

STATE BIRD: loon

STATE FLOWER: pink and white lady's slipper

STATE TREE: Norway pine

STATE CAPITAL: St. Paul

AREA: 86,939 sq mi (225,172 sq km)

You're bound to find whatever floats your boat in Minnesota, home to more lakes than any state except Alaska. Trade in your car for a canoe and you'll never grow tired of exploring the wet wilds—even when wintertime calls for exploration on ice skates and sleds.

Roadside Attractions

A HUGE BALL OF TWINE
A 13-foot (4-m) boulder of solid twine in Darwin has become an icon of oddball roadside attractions.

SOUDAN UNDERGROUND MINE
Don a hard hat and ride an elevator half a mile (0.8 km) underground to an old iron mine.

PAUL BUNYAN AND BABE THE OX
Tall tales don't get any taller than those of Paul Bunyan, the mythical lumberjack who created Minnesota's lakes with his boot prints. See towering statues of this larger-than-life folk hero and his blue-hued sidekick in Bemidji.

FANTASTIC MINNESOTA FACTS

The "Land of 10,000 Lakes" nickname shortchanges the state by a few thousand lakes.

Even in the dead of winter, people in Minneapolis can get around town wearing short sleeves. The city has a network of heated tunnels!

Waterskiing was invented in Minnesota in 1922.

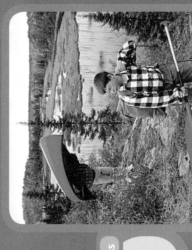

5 COOL THINGS TO DO HERE

1 WOLVES
Voyageurs National Park

Listen for the howl of the timber wolf when you visit this watery wilderness. It's a sanctuary for the secretive animals.

2 CANOEING
Boundary Waters Canoe Area Wilderness

Motorboats are not allowed on most lakes in this vast expanse of forest-fringed streams and lakes, a paradise for paddlers.

CANADA

RED LAKE IND. RES.

Lake of the Woods

12 59 75

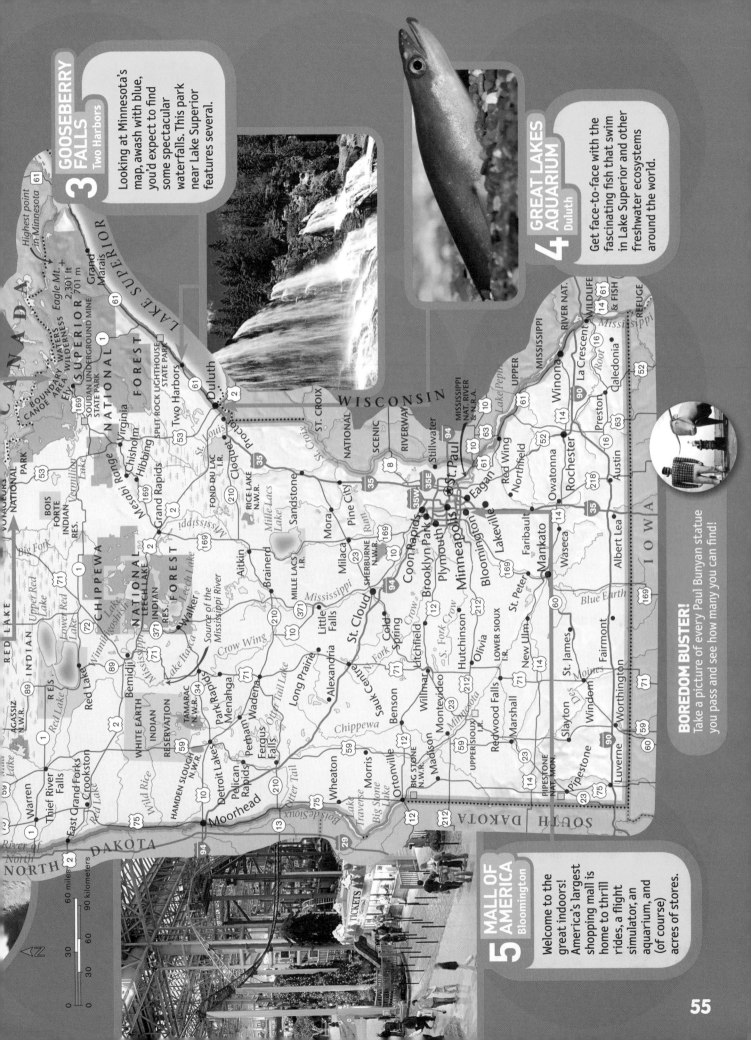

3 GOOSEBERRY FALLS
Two Harbors

Looking at Minnesota's map, awash with blue, you'd expect to find some spectacular waterfalls. This park near Lake Superior features several.

4 GREAT LAKES AQUARIUM
Duluth

Get face-to-face with the fascinating fish that swim in Lake Superior and other freshwater ecosystems around the world.

5 MALL OF AMERICA
Bloomington

Welcome to the great indoors! America's largest shopping mall is home to thrill rides, a flight simulator, an aquarium, and (of course) acres of stores.

BOREDOM BUSTER!
Take a picture of every Paul Bunyan statue you pass and see how many you can find!

CANADA

Highest point in Minnesota

Eagle Mt. 2,301 ft + 701 m

Grand Marais

LAKE SUPERIOR

BOUNDARY WATERS CANOE AREA WILDERNESS

SOUDAN UNDERGROUND MINE

SPLIT ROCK LIGHTHOUSE STATE PARK

Ely

Grand Rapids

Virginia

Chisholm

Hibbing

Mesabi Range

VOYAGEURS NATIONAL PARK

BOIS FORTE INDIAN RES.

Vermilion Lake

NATIONAL FOREST

CHIPPEWA

Two Harbors

Duluth

WISCONSIN

St. Louis

Proctor

Cloquet

FOND DU LAC I.R.

Sandstone

RICE LAKE N.W.R.

Mille Lacs Lake

Mora

Pine City

Rush Lake

ST. CROIX NATIONAL SCENIC RIVERWAY

Stillwater

St. Paul

MISSISSIPPI NAT. RIVER & N.R.A.

Red Wing

Lake Pepin

UPPER MISSISSIPPI RIVER NAT. WILDLIFE & FISH REFUGE

Winona

La Crescent

Caledonia

Root

Preston

Austin

Rochester

Owatonna

Northfield

Faribault

Eagan

Minneapolis

Bloomington

Lakeville

Mankato

Waseca

St. Peter

Blue Earth

Albert Lea

IOWA

Coon Rapids

Brooklyn Park

Plymouth

St. Cloud

Milaca

SHERBURNE N.W.R.

MILLE LACS I.R.

Aitkin

Brainerd

Little Falls

Crow Wing

Source of the Mississippi River

Lake Itasca

Walker

Bemidji

LEECH LAKE INDIAN RES.

Leech Lake

Winnibigoshish L.

NATIONAL FOREST

RED LAKE INDIAN RES.

Red Lake

Upper Red Lake

Lower Red Lake

Big Fork

AGASSIZ N.W.R.

Thief River Falls

Warren

Crookston

East Grand Forks

River of the North

NORTH DAKOTA

Moorhead

Detroit Lakes

Pelican Rapids

Fergus Falls

Wild Rice

WHITE EARTH INDIAN RESERVATION

TAMARAC N.W.R.

Park Rapids

Menahga

Wadena

Perham

Otter Tail Lake

HAMDEN SLOUGH N.W.R.

Red Lake

Long Prairie

Alexandria

Sauk Centre

Willmar

Litchfield

Hutchinson

Olivia

Redwood Falls

Marshall

Montevideo

Madison

Benson

Morris

Wheaton

Ortonville

Big Stone Lake

BIG STONE N.W.R.

UPPER SIOUX I.R.

LOWER SIOUX I.R.

New Ulm

St. James

Windom

Worthington

Fairmont

Des Moines

Luverne

Pipestone

PIPESTONE NAT. MON.

Slayton

Chippewa

Minnesota

Crow

S. Fork Crow

Cold Spring

Cottonwood

Mississippi

Bois de Sioux

Lake Traverse

Big Sioux

Otter Tail

SOUTH DAKOTA

WISCONSIN

N

60 miles

90 kilometers

55

STATE BIRD: mockingbird

STATE FLOWER: magnolia

STATE ANIMAL: white-tailed deer

STATE CAPITAL: Jackson
AREA: 48,430 sq mi (125,434 sq km)

MISSISSIPPI
The Magnolia State

You won't get the whole Mississippi experience if you tour just its casino steamboats, scenic byways, and pre–Civil War plantations. This state must be heard as well as seen! Blues music, born on the banks of the Mississippi, is a vital part of any excursion to this Deep South state.

Roadside Attractions

BIRTHPLACE OF KERMIT THE FROG
Kermit creator Jim Henson was born in Leland, where you'll find an exhibit honoring the man and his Muppets at the chamber of commerce.

COCA-COLA MUSEUM
This restored candy store in Vicksburg sits where, in 1894, Coca-Cola was first bottled. See the original bottling equipment while slurping down ice-cream floats.

GROUND ZERO HURRICANE MUSEUM
At this unique museum in Waveland, the display of Katrina Recovery Quilts, made with restored fabrics found after the hurricane, weaves together stories about the storm's human impact.

FANTASTIC MISSISSIPPI FACTS

Most of the nation's farm-raised catfish comes from Belzoni.

Legendary blues guitarist B.B. King was born near Itta Bena.

Theodore "Teddy" Roosevelt's refusal to shoot a bear in Mississippi inspired the creation of the teddy bear.

5 COOL THINGS TO DO HERE

1 DELTA BLUES
Clarksdale

Soak in the soulful sounds of Mississippi blues music at the Delta Blues Museum.

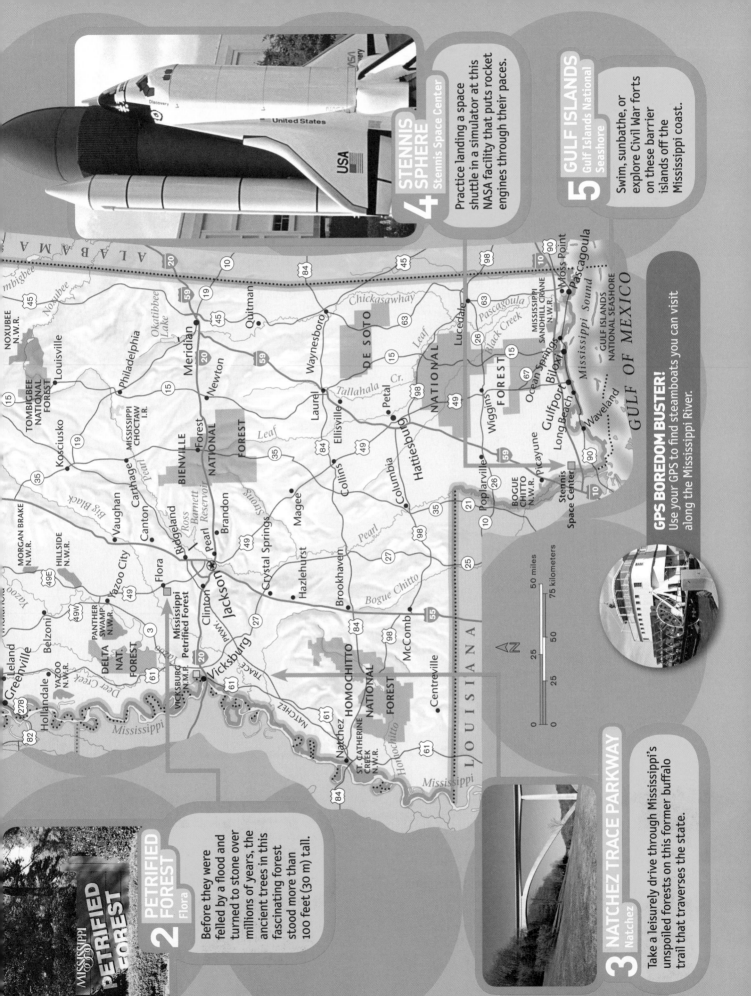

4 STENNIS SPHERE
Stennis Space Center

Practice landing a space shuttle in a simulator at this NASA facility that puts rocket engines through their paces.

5 GULF ISLANDS
Gulf Islands National Seashore

Swim, sunbathe, or explore Civil War forts on these barrier islands off the Mississippi coast.

2 PETRIFIED FOREST
Flora

Before they were felled by a flood and turned to stone over millions of years, the ancient trees in this fascinating forest stood more than 100 feet (30 m) tall.

3 NATCHEZ TRACE PARKWAY
Natchez

Take a leisurely drive through Mississippi's unspoiled forests on this former buffalo trail that traverses the state.

GPS BOREDOM BUSTER!
Use your GPS to find steamboats you can visit along the Mississippi River.

5 COOL THINGS TO DO HERE

0 25 50 miles
0 25 50 75 kilometers

N

1 PONY EXPRESS MUSEUM
St. Joseph

Discover a newfound appreciation for modern technology when you learn about the lightning-fast riders who carried letters from this railroad outpost all the way to California in the early 1860s.

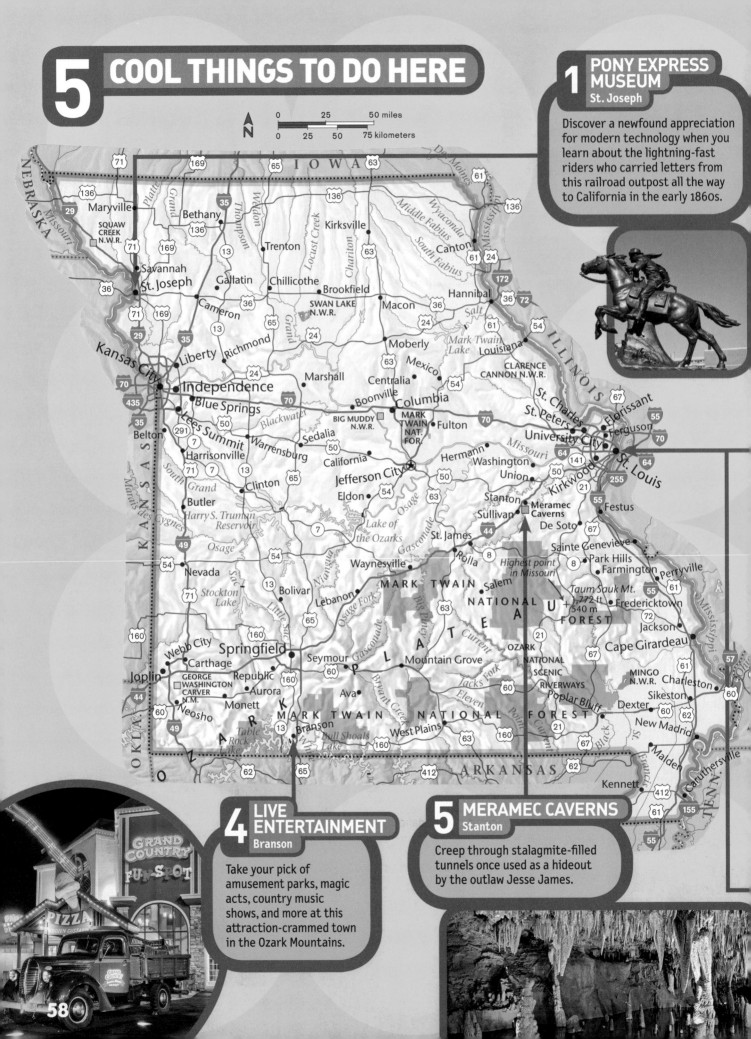

4 LIVE ENTERTAINMENT
Branson

Take your pick of amusement parks, magic acts, country music shows, and more at this attraction-crammed town in the Ozark Mountains.

5 MERAMEC CAVERNS
Stanton

Creep through stalagmite-filled tunnels once used as a hideout by the outlaw Jesse James.

 **STATE BIRD:** bluebird

 STATE FLOWER: white hawthorn

 STATE ANIMAL: Missouri mule

 STATE CAPITAL: Jefferson City
AREA: 69,704 sq mi (180,534 sq km)

MISSOURI
The Show-Me STATE

When explorers Meriwether Lewis and William Clark set out to chart the American West in 1804, they used Missouri as their launching point. A sense of adventure has thrived in this "gateway to the West" ever since.

FANTASTIC MISSOURI FACTS

Hundreds of species of grasses grow on Missouri's prairies.

Kansas City has more than 200 fountains.

Square dancing is the official state folk dance.

2 GATEWAY ARCH
St. Louis

Squeeze into a tiny tram and ride to the top of this 630-foot (192-m) steel monument to America's pioneering spirit.

3 CITY MUSEUM
St. Louis

Scramble around a dream jungle gym made of fighter jets, fire engines, and oversize Slinky toys suspended 25 feet (7.6 m) high!

Roadside Attractions

MARK TWAIN CAVE
The famous author chased bats in this creepy cavern while growing up in Hannibal. He later used it as a setting in *The Adventures of Tom Sawyer*.

GRANT'S FARM
Zebra, antelope, and other exotic animals roam this St. Louis safari park.

TITANIC MUSEUM
It's hard to miss Branson's ship-shaped museum for the doomed passenger liner.

BOREDOM BUSTER!
Missouri once raised more mules (for its westbound wagon trains) than any other state. See how many mules you can capture with your camera today!

59

STATE BIRD: western meadowlark

STATE FLOWER: bitterroot

STATE ANIMAL: grizzly bear

STATE CAPITAL: Helena
AREA: 147,042 sq mi (380,840 sq km)

MONTANA
The BIG SKY COUNTRY

Seeing why Montana is nick-named Big Sky Country is easy: Just look up! A canopy of blue stretches from horizon to horizon over the wide-open prairies in the east and the snowcapped Rocky Mountains in the west. Don't look up too long, though—Big Sky Country is also grizzly bear country!

WHAT A SILLY SIGN!

Bad Route Road off Inter-state 94 in Montana's eastern prairieland doesn't sound like the most inviting road trip detour, but at least it has a rest area!

EXIT 192
Bad Route Road
1 MILE
REST AREA

Roadside Attractions

SMOKEJUMPERS BASE
Meet Missoula's brave daredevils: the men and women of the Aerial Fire Depot in Missoula who jump out of planes to battle remote forest blazes.

WORLD'S LARGEST STEER
A two-ton (1.8-t) bovine named Steer Montana became the state's hottest hoofed celebrity in the 1920s. See his stuffed body at the O'Fallon Historical Society Museum in Baker.

45TH PARALLEL MARKER
A plain wooden sign near the north entrance of Yellowstone National Park is positioned about halfway between the Equator and the North Pole.

3 VIRGINIA CITY
Virginia City

Pan for gold in this pioneer ghost town, unchanged for 150 years.

BOREDOM BUSTER!
Snap pics of the Rocky Mountains and Montana's wide-open prairies. Print them out as Big Sky Country postcards when you get home!

5 COOL THINGS TO DO HERE

1 GRIZZLY BEARS
Glacier National Park

Big solitary beasts dwell in the forests, meadows, and glacier-carved valleys of Montana's most beautiful park. Keep your distance, though—grizzlies are no teddy bears!

2 BEARTOOTH HIGHWAY
Red Lodge

Brave perilous switchbacks and summer snowstorms as you drive up, up, and up this breathtaking stretch of high-altitude highway in the Rocky Mountains.

4 BIG SKY RESORT
Big Sky

Conquer a nearly endless supply of ski runs in the winter, or zoom along daredevil bike trails in the summer, at this all-season resort.

5 LITTLE BIGHORN
Crow Agency

Tour the battlefield where Lt. Col. George Armstrong Custer made his famous last stand against Plains Native American warriors.

NEBRASKA
The Cornhusker STATE

C ornfields and cattle ranches sprawl in every direction in this Great Plains state. In fact, 91 percent of Nebraska's land area is made up of farms and ranches. But there is much more to see here. The state is also home to many natural wonders and fantastically fun attractions.

FANTASTIC NEBRASKA FACTS

Thousands of letters pass through the small wilderness town of Valentine each February 14 to get postmarked with its lovey-dovey name.

Chimney Rock, a 300-foot (91.4-m) sandstone spire near Bayard, was the most famous landmark along the Oregon Trail. Westbound pioneers often drew pictures of it in their journals.

Nebraska is the only U.S. state with a unicameral legislature (meaning just one branch). Every other state has a bicameral, or two-branch, legislative system.

Roadside Attractions

CARHENGE
England's prehistoric Stonehenge monument is re-created near the town of Alliance—with 38 gray-painted vintage automobiles instead of rock slabs.

NATIONAL MUSEUM OF ROLLER SKATING
This small brick building in Lincoln is home to the world's biggest collection of roller skates, including jet-powered skates!

STRATEGIC AIR & SPACE MUSEUM
Visit this aircraft hangar in Ashland to make an up-close inspection of more than 30 fighter jets and cargo planes.

BOREDOM BUSTER!
Take a picture of every upturned boot you pass on a fence post—a common cowboy-approved ranch decoration—and see how many you can find!

5 COOL THINGS TO DO HERE

1 SCOTTS BLUFF
Gering

Hike to the 800-foot (244-m) summit of this sandstone bluff that marked the trail for Pony Express riders and pioneers traveling west. You can still see their wagonwheel ruts 150 years later!

2 SANDHILLS
North-Central Nebraska

Take a stroll through one of the world's geological oddities: a sea of grass-carpeted sand dunes covering a quarter of Nebraska.

3 HENRY DOORLY ZOO AND AQUARIUM
Omaha

Stand within the habitats of gorillas, lemurs, and creatures of the night in this amazing zoo that immerses visitors in its animal kingdoms.

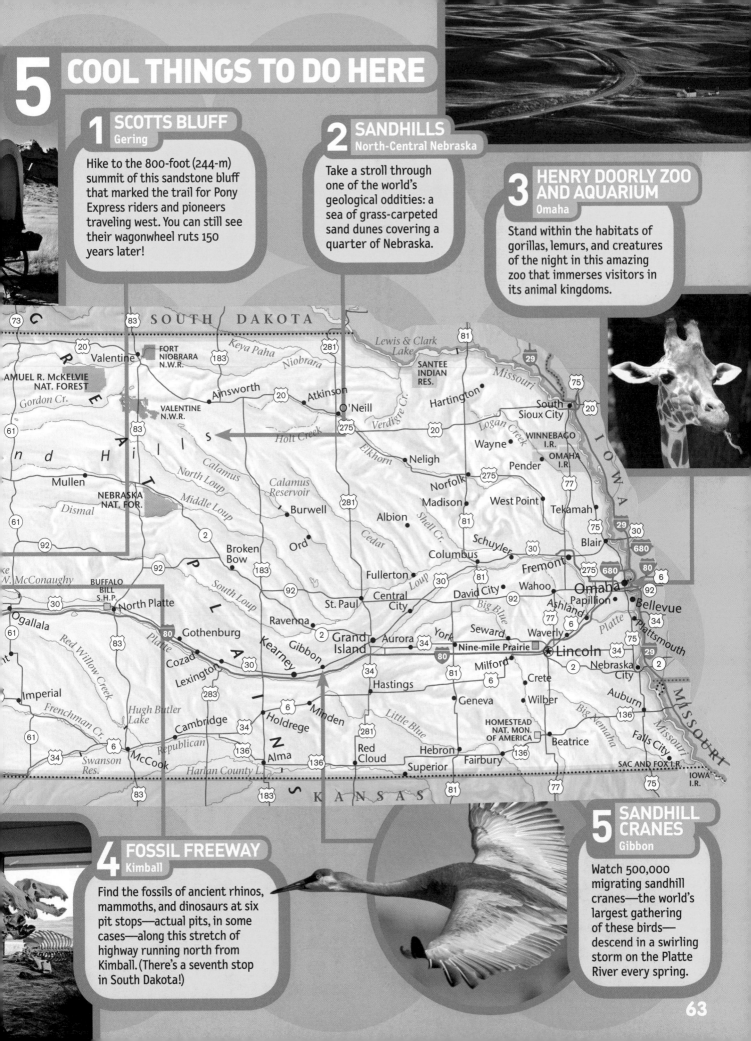

SOUTH DAKOTA

SAMUEL R. McKELVIE NAT. FOREST

NEBRASKA NAT. FOR.

BUFFALO BILL S.H.P.

HOMESTEAD NAT. MON. OF AMERICA

KANSAS

IOWA

MISSOURI

4 FOSSIL FREEWAY
Kimball

Find the fossils of ancient rhinos, mammoths, and dinosaurs at six pit stops—actual pits, in some cases—along this stretch of highway running north from Kimball. (There's a seventh stop in South Dakota!)

5 SANDHILL CRANES
Gibbon

Watch 500,000 migrating sandhill cranes—the world's largest gathering of these birds—descend in a swirling storm on the Platte River every spring.

NEVADA
The Silver STATE

STATE BIRD: mountain bluebird

STATE FLOWER: sagebrush

STATE ANIMAL: desert bighorn

STATE CAPITAL: Carson City
AREA: 110,561 sq mi (286,352 sq km)

From the 19th-century miners who struck silver near Reno to the lucky gamblers who win big in Las Vegas' rowdy casinos today, visitors to Nevada have a habit of hitting the jackpot.

With a lot of attractions geared toward grown-ups, will kids find any fun stuff here? It's a safe bet.

WHAT A SILLY SIGN!

EXTRATERRESTRIAL HIGHWAY 375

Watch the skies as well as Route 375 when you pass this spaced-out sign near Rachel, Nevada. The state officially designated this 98-mile (158-km) byway as the "Extraterrestrial Highway" after so many motorists reported UFO sightings. The military's super-secret Area 51 airbase is also nearby. Coincidence?

Roadside Attractions

> **LAS VEGAS NATURAL HISTORY MUSEUM**
This family-friendly and popular museum features a *T. rex* and a shark-infested coral reef.

> **VIRGINIA CITY**
This Wild West boomtown looks just like it did more than 150 years ago, when prospectors struck silver.

> **FLY GEYSER**
Check out this cool geyser in the Black Rock desert just north of Gerlach. This mighty mound looks out of this world due to the colorful algae that has formed on its surface.

5 COOL THINGS TO DO HERE

1 LAKE TAHOE
Lake Tahoe Nevada State Park

One of America's largest, deepest, and bluest bodies of water, mountain-ringed Lake Tahoe is a paradise for boaters in the summer and ski bums in the winter.

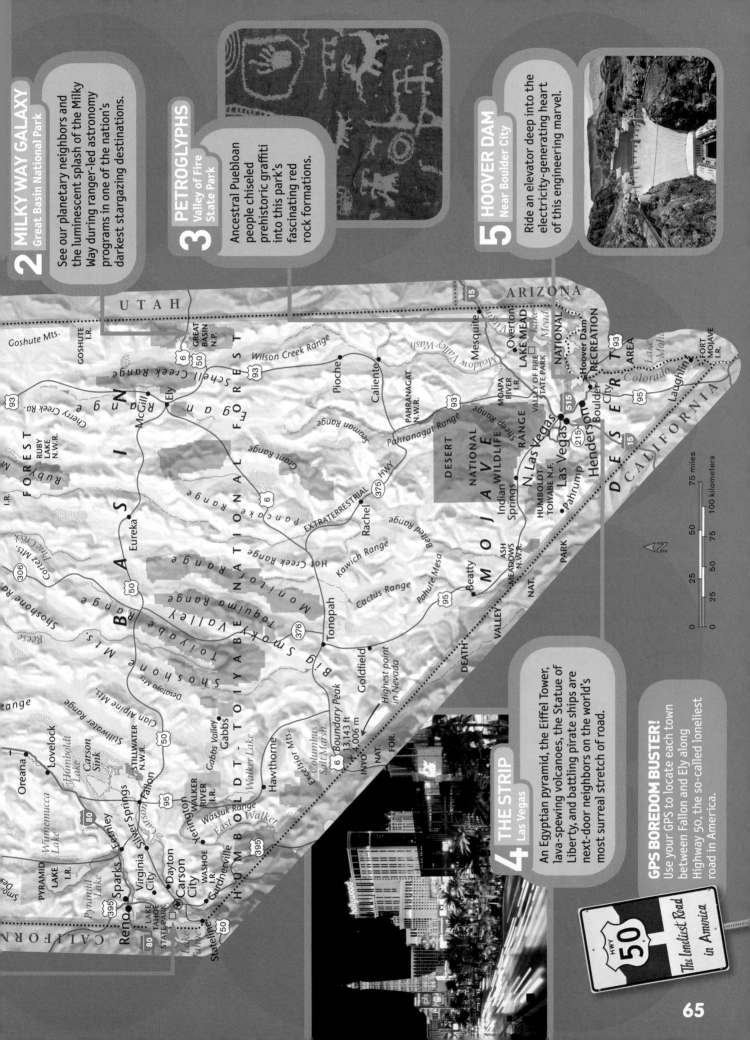

2 MILKY WAY GALAXY
Great Basin National Park

See our planetary neighbors and the luminescent splash of the Milky Way during ranger-led astronomy programs in one of the nation's darkest stargazing destinations.

3 PETROGLYPHS
Valley of Fire State Park

Ancestral Puebloan people chiseled prehistoric graffiti into this park's fascinating red rock formations.

5 HOOVER DAM
Near Boulder City

Ride an elevator deep into the electricity-generating heart of this engineering marvel.

4 THE STRIP
Las Vegas

An Egyptian pyramid, the Eiffel Tower, lava-spewing volcanoes, the Statue of Liberty, and battling pirate ships are next-door neighbors on the world's most surreal stretch of road.

GPS BOREDOM BUSTER!

Use your GPS to locate each town between Fallon and Ely along Highway 50, the so-called loneliest road in America.

50 HWY
The Loneliest Road in America

Map labels

UTAH

ARIZONA

Goshute Mts.
GOSHUTE I.R.
GREAT BASIN N.P.
Wilson Creek Range
Schell Creek Range
Cherry Creek Ra.
Egan Range
RUBY LAKE N.W.R.
Ruby Mts.
FOREST
GREAT BASIN
McGill
Ely
Pioche
Caliente
PAHRANAGAT N.W.R.
Pahranagat Range
Seaman Range
Giant Range
EXTRATERRESTRIAL HWY
Rachel
Hot Creek Range
Pancake Range
Eureka
Monitor Range
Cortez Mts.
Pine Creek
Reese River
Shoshone Mts.
Toiyabe Range
Toquima Range
Big Smoky Valley
HUMBOLDT-TOIYABE NATIONAL FOREST
Kawich Range
Cactus Range
Belted Range
Pahute Mesa
Beatty
DESERT NATIONAL WILDLIFE RANGE
Sheep Range
Indian Springs
N. Las Vegas
Las Vegas
Henderson
Boulder City
Hoover Dam
LAKE MEAD NATIONAL RECREATION AREA
Lake Mead
Overton
VALLEY OF FIRE STATE PARK
Mesquite
Virgin River
Meadow Valley Wash
MOAPA RIVER I.R.
HUMBOLDT-TOIYABE N.F.
Pahrump
ASH MEADOWS N.W.R.
MOJAVE NATIONAL PRESERVE
DEATH VALLEY NAT. PARK
INYO NAT. FOR.
Boundary Peak 13,143 ft 4,006 m
Highest point in Nevada
Goldfield
Tonopah
Gabbs
Gabbs Valley
Excelsior Mts.
Columbus Salt Marsh
Hawthorne
Walker Lake
Wassuk Range
East Walker
Walker River I.R.
WALKER RIVER I.R.
Yerington
Fallon
STILLWATER N.W.R.
Carson Sink
Humboldt Lake
Stillwater Range
Clan Alpine Mts.
Desatoya Mts.
Shoshone Range
Cortez Mts.
Lovelock
Oreana
Winnemucca Lake
Pyramid Lake
PYRAMID LAKE I.R.
Reno
Sparks
Fernley
Virginia City
Dayton
Carson City
LAKE TAHOE STATE PARK
Lake Tahoe
Stateline
Gardnerville
WASHOE I.R.
CALIFORNIA
MOJAVE DESERT
Colorado River
Lake Mohave
FORT MOJAVE I.R.
Laughlin

Scale

0 25 50 75 miles
0 25 50 75 100 kilometers

N

NEW HAMPSHIRE

The Granite STATE

STATE CAPITAL: Concord
AREA: 9,350 sq mi (24,216 sq km)

STATE ANIMAL: white-tailed deer

STATE FLOWER: purple lilac

STATE BIRD: purple finch

S pend a week exploring this picturesque state and you'll wind up jealous of the moose that get to live here year-round.

Dazzling fall foliage, crystal lakes, granite peaks, country hamlets—everything people love about New England is here in New Hampshire.

Roadside Attractions

→ **AMERICAN CLASSIC ARCADE MUSEUM**
The bleeps and blips of vintage video games are preserved forever at this museum that lets you play with the exhibits. Find it in Laconia's Funspot Family Fun Center, the self-proclaimed world's largest arcade!

→ **AMERICA'S STONEHENGE**
Salem is home to a human-made stone construction of walls, chambers, and meeting places for ceremonies. Who built it? No one knows for sure, but what is known is that the ancient stones make up an accurate astronomical calendar!

→ **WILDCAT MOUNTAIN ZIPRIDER**
Visit this ski resort near Pinkham Notch in the summer for a zooming zip line ride over spectacular mountain scenery at 45 miles an hour (72 km/h)!

WHAT A SILLY SIGN!

BRAKE FOR MOOSE
IT COULD SAVE YOUR LIFE
HUNDREDS OF COLLISIONS

The "Brake for Moose" signs in northern New Hampshire may seem a little silly, but their message is no joke! Colliding with one of these half-ton (45-t) animals is like ramming into a six-foot (1.8-m) brick wall—with antlers! Look for their long faces poking from the sides of the roads, and use high beams at night to see the gleam of moose eyeballs.

5 COOL THINGS TO DO HERE

1 MOOSE
Pittsburg

About 3,500 of these six-foot (1.8-m)-tall animals roam New Hampshire's forests. The best moose-spotting is along a stretch of Route 3 north of Pittsburg called "Moose Alley."

CANADA

Third L.

First Connecticut Lake

Second Lake

257

3

Pittsburg

Lake Francis

114

Colebrook

26

Blue Mt.
3,723 ft
1,135 m

North Stratford

Connecticut

LAKE UMBAGOG N.W.R.

Umbagog L.

Andros

16

2 FLUME GORGE
Lincoln

Delve into a 90-foot (27-m)-deep glacier-carved gorge to see a series of spectacular waterfalls.

3 KANCAMAGUS HIGHWAY
White Mountain National Forest

Cruise alongside icy mountain rivers and over granite ridges on this 34-mile (55-km) scenic roadway, which offers unparalleled vistas of New England's famous fall foliage.

4 COG RAILWAY
Mount Washington

Chug above the clouds to the summit of New England's tallest mountain on this steam-powered train built in 1869.

5 PORTSMOUTH HARBOR
Portsmouth

Walk the Portsmouth Harbor Trail to see the 18th- and 19th-century buildings of this postcard-perfect New England fishing village.

BOREDOM BUSTER!

"Old Man on the Mountain," a famous face-shaped rock formation in the White Mountains, collapsed in 2003. Scrutinize any granite ridges you pass for a replacement.

Oldest covered bridge in New Hampshire (1829)

Highest point in New Hampshire

MAINE

VERMONT

MASSACHUSETTS

CONNECTICUT

WHITE MOUNTAIN NATIONAL FOREST

APPALACHIAN MTS.

Presidential Range

Mt. Washington 6,288 ft 1,917 m

Mt. Lafayette 5,249 ft 1,600 m

Mt. Sunapee 2,743 ft 836 m

Monadnock Mt. 3,165 ft 965 m

SAINT-GAUDENS NATIONAL HISTORIC SITE

President Pierce's birthplace

WAPACK N.W.R.

PISGAH S.P.

MT. SUNAPEE S.P.

FRANCONIA NOTCH S.P.

CRAWFORD NOTCH S.P.

67

NEW JERSEY

The Garden STATE

T he "Garden State" of New Jersey doesn't live up to its nickname if you see it solely from the traffic-jammed New Jersey Turnpike. Find greener pastures—literally—away from the interstate, along with lots of fun in the sun.

STATE CAPITAL: Trenton
AREA: 8,721 sq mi (22,588 sq km)

STATE ANIMAL: horse

STATE FLOWER: purple violet

STATE BIRD: eastern goldfinch

FANTASTIC NEW JERSEY FACTS

You're not allowed to pump your own gas in the Garden State.

More Revolutionary War battles were fought in New Jersey than in any other state.

The first organized baseball game was played in Hoboken in 1846.

Roadside Attractions

LUCY THE ELEPHANT
Built in 1881, this elephant-shaped house in Margate City has become a Jersey Shore icon.

DISCOVERY SEASHELL MUSEUM
Prepare to be shell-shocked when you visit this Ocean City museum crammed with thousands of seashells from around the world.

HUGE SPOON COLLECTION
If being a medieval fortress in the New Jersey countryside isn't strange enough, Paterson's Lambert Castle is also home to a very large spoon collection!

5 COOL THINGS TO DO HERE

1 DUKE FARMS Hillsborough

See how the Garden State got its nickname when you tour the greenhouses and lush grounds of this sprawling estate.

4 INSECTROPOLIS
Toms River

Meet every kind of creepy crawler at this big bug zoo.

MOST faze wings

5 THE BOARDWALK
Atlantic City

Find all the thrill rides and deep-fried funnel cakes you can stomach at this rowdy stretch of the Jersey Shore—the inspiration for the Monopoly game board.

GPS BOREDOM BUSTER!
Use your GPS to count all the boardwalk amusement parks along the Jersey Shore.

2 ADVENTURE AQUARIUM
Camden

Scratch sharks behind the gills and feed stingrays by hand. Don't forget to say hello to the hippos!

3 CAPE MAY
Cape May

Walk along a serene stretch of the Jersey Shore in this old-fashioned beach town full of quaint cottages and historic inns.

Map labels

OCEAN
ATLANTIC

Electric light invented by Thomas Edison, 1879

Sandy Hook
GATEWAY N.R.A.
Long Branch
Asbury Park
Belmar
Manasquan
Point Pleasant
Gilford Park
Seaside Heights

Eatontown
Red Bank
Cheesequake
Keansburg
Freehold
Neptune
Lakewood
Lakehurst
Crestwood Village

Perth Amboy
Rahway
Elizabeth
Plainfield
Menlo Park
Edison
New Brunswick
East Brunswick
Sayreville
Kendall Park
Piscataway
Somerville
Hillsborough
Flemington
Lambertville
Princeton

Raritan
Manalapan
Delaware & Raritan Canal

Mount Holly
Hightstown
Mercerville
White Horse
Trenton
Ewing
Burlington
Willingboro
Cinnaminson
Pennsauken
Camden
Paulsboro
Penns Grove
Pennsville
Salem

Browns Mills
Double Trouble
Toms River

First dinosaur skeleton discovered in North America, 1858

Haddonfield
Cherry Hill
Woodbury
Lindenwold
Pine Hill
Glassboro
Williamstown
Woodstown
Vineland
Bridgeton
Millville
Woodbine

PINE BARRENS
Toms
Barnegat Bay
Long Beach Island
Surf City
Ship Bottom
Little Egg Harbor
Beach Haven
Mystic Island
Great Bay

E.B. FORSYTHE N.W.R.
Mullica
Egg Harbor City
Hammonton
ATLANTIC CITY
Mays Landing
Absecon
Brigantine
Atlantic City
Ventnor City
Margate City
Ocean City
Somers Point
Tuckahoe
Sea Isle City

Great Egg Harbor
GARDEN STATE PARKWAY
EXPRESSWAY
Maurice
SUPAWNA MEADOWS N.W.R.
Salem
Cohansey
Delaware Bay
Delaware

CAPE MAY
Cape May Court House
North Wildwood
Wildwood
Cape May
Cape May Canal

PENNSYLVANIA
Delaware
Round Valley Res.

DELAWARE

NEW JERSEY

Route numbers: 278, 287, 18, 9, 195, 95, 206, 1, 295, 276, 70, 40, 55, 49, 47, 347, 83, 9

Scale: 20 miles / 30 kilometers

69

NEW MEXICO

Land of Enchantment

From the pastel mesas that dominate the desert to the mud-colored adobe homes of the suburbs, New Mexico's landscape is inescapable. The first Native American residents became one with the rugged terrain, too, creating palaces in the sandstone cliffs deep in the heart of the stark Southwest.

STATE BIRD: roadrunner

STATE FLOWER: yucca

STATE ANIMAL: black bear

STATE CAPITAL: Santa Fe
AREA: 121,590 sq mi (314,917 sq km)

FANTASTIC NEW MEXICO FACTS

Generations of Native Americans have lived in an adobe house in Taos for more than 1,000 years, making it the country's oldest continuously inhabited building.

The northwest corner of New Mexico is the only border spot where you can stand in four states simultaneously.

Infamous outlaw Billy the Kid has two graves at Fort Sumner, where he was gunned down at age 22. Neither grave is real, although one sports his true tombstone.

Roadside Attractions

➤ UFO MUSEUM
The U.S. government denies that an alien spaceship crashed in Roswell in 1947. Investigate the incident for yourself at the International UFO Museum and Research Center.

➤ ICE CAVE
Need a break from the New Mexico heat? Take a refreshing hike into a perpetually icy cave at the Bandera Volcano, near Grants.

➤ BRADBURY SCIENCE MUSEUM
Try fun science experiments and learn about the race to build the atomic bomb in this museum at the Los Alamos National Laboratory.

5 COOL THINGS TO DO HERE

1 SKY CITY
Acoma Pueblo

Explore this Native American town set atop a 367-foot (112-m) sheer-walled mesa, established 450 years before the first English colonies.

2 PUYE CLIFF DWELLINGS
Española

Every room has a view in this mile-long (1.6-km) village that was cut into a cliff face over a thousand years ago by the Native American Pueblo people.

Only spot in the U.S. where the borders of four states come together

Four Corners
UTE MOUNTAIN I. R.
Shiprock
Farmington
Bloomfield
Navajo Reservoir
Dulce
Chama
COLORADO
Highest point in New Mexico
Raton
CAPULIN VOLCANO N.M.
Dry Cimarron
Cimarron
Rio Grande
OK
64
550
84
285
522

3 SANDIA PEAK TRAMWAY
Albuquerque

Ascend 4,000 feet (1.2 km) in 15 minutes for a panoramic view of New Mexico's rugged and varied landscape.

4 BATS
Carlsbad Caverns

Watch thousands of Mexican free-tailed bats swarm out of Carlsbad Caverns each summer night in search of yummy bugs.

5 WHITE SANDS
Near Alamogordo

It may look like a winter wonderland, but the White Sands National Monument is actually the world's largest white gypsum desert. Come in the summer for a midnight hike under a full moon!

BOREDOM BUSTER!

As you ride through the state's beige terrain, keep your eyes peeled for a flash of blue—it's a mountain bluebird! Try to snap a photo of one.

TEXAS

MEXICO

ARIZONA

LLANO ESTACADO

ROCKY MOUNTAINS

Largest natural underground chamber in North America

Site of first atomic bomb test, July 16, 1945

 **STATE BIRD:** bluebird

 **STATE FLOWER:** rose

STATE ANIMAL: beaver

STATE CAPITAL: Albany
AREA: 54,556 sq mi (141,300 sq km)

NEW YORK

The Empire STATE

Roadside Attractions

N ew York is best known for its vibrant city of skyscrapers and bustling sidewalks, but outside New York City lies a serene landscape of lakes, mountains, and waterfalls. From wild urban adventures to quiet beach walks at sunrise, the Empire State has an activity for everyone.

NATIONAL BASEBALL HALL OF FAME

See how America's pastime has evolved over time in this Cooperstown shrine to the sport.

CONEY ISLAND

Pig out on hot dogs, then try not to lose your lunch on the thrill rides at this historic boardwalk amusement park in Brooklyn.

SECRET CAVERNS

You'll know you're getting close to this 100-foot (30.5-m) subterranean waterfall east of Cobleskill when you spy its famously funky hand-painted billboards.

FANTASTIC NEW YORK FACTS

Bean bags can only be tossed in designated areas within the parks of the town of Hempstead.

Flirting on the streets of New York City could cost you a $25 fine.

It's illegal in New York City to walk around with an ice-cream cone in your pocket on Sundays.

BOREDOM BUSTER!
New York City is home to movie stars and famous musicians. Look for celebrities out and about—and keep your camera handy!

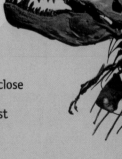

5 COOL THINGS TO DO HERE

1 MAID OF THE MIST
Niagara Falls State Park

Don a raincoat and embark on a wet and wild boat ride along the base of the mightiest waterfall in America.

2 ADIRONDACK PARK
Northern New York

Hike, raft, or ride through the largest state park in the U.S., a lush wilderness of mountains, rivers, and secret lakes.

3 CATSKILL MOUNTAINS
Catskill Park

Hunt for hidden waterfalls and explore quaint resort towns in this mountainous forest, a retreat for city slickers seeking a breath of fresh air.

4 NIGHTTIME TOUR
New York City

Grab a flashlight and take a nocturnal tour of the American Museum of Natural History, the famous setting for the film *Night at the Museum*.

5 EMPIRE STATE BUILDING
New York City

Enjoy a bird's-eye view of the Statue of Liberty and the Brooklyn Bridge from the 86th floor of the Big Apple's iconic skyscraper.

Map labels

CANADA

St. Lawrence · ST. REGIS I.R. · Massena · Malone · Dannemora · Plattsburgh · Ogdensburg · Potsdam · Morristown · Saranac Lake · Lake Champlain · Gouverneur · Lake Placid · Thousand Islands · Raquette · Mt. Marcy 5,344 ft 1,629 m · Highest point in New York · Ticonderoga · Watertown · Black · ADIRONDACK · Fort Ticonderoga · Lake George · Lowville · Mountains · PARK · VERMONT · Warrensburg · Oswego · Fulton · FORT STANWIX N.M. · Oneida Lake · Rome · Little Falls · Great Sacandaga Lake · Glens Falls · LAKE ONTARIO · Irondequoit · Fairmount · Oneida · Utica · Gloversville · Saratoga Springs · SARATOGA N.H.P. · Rochester · MONTEZUMA N.W.R. · Syracuse · Ilion · Amsterdam · Schenectady · Auburn · Mohawk · Niskayuna · Canandaigua · Geneva · Seneca Falls · Seneca L. · Cooperstown · Cobleskill · Troy · Finger Lakes · Cortland · Albany · Kinderhook · Penn Yan · Cayuga Lake · Norwich · APPALACHIAN MOUNTAINS · MARTIN VAN BUREN N.H.S. · NEW YORK STATE THRUWAY · Keuka Lake · FINGER LAKES NAT. FOR. · Ithaca · Oneonta · Sidney · Catskill · Hudson · Bath · Watkins Glen · Delaware · Catskill Mountains · Kingston · Taconic Range · Horseheads · Endwell · Binghamton · CATSKILL PARK · Slide Mt. 4,180 ft 1,274 m · Elmira · Endicott · Susquehanna · W. Branch Delaware · MASS. · Corning · E. Branch · HOME OF FRANKLIN D. ROOSEVELT N.H.S. · Wellsville · PENNSYLVANIA · Monticello · New Paltz · TACONIC STATE PARKWAY · CONN. · NAT. · Newburgh · Poughkeepsie · APPALACHIAN TRAIL · Middletown · West Point · Beacon · Port Jervis · U.S. Military Academy · Peekskill · R.I. · Block Island Sound · Spring Valley · New City · White Plains · Long Island Sound · Montauk Point · Tuxedo Park · Tarrytown · Huntington · Sag Harbor · Yonkers · Long Island · Coram · Southampton · New York · Brooklyn · Centereach · Hempstead · FIRE ISLAND NATIONAL SEASHORE · Ellis Island · Freeport · Statue of Liberty · Long Beach · ATLANTIC OCEAN · Staten Island · Coney Island · N.J. · Delaware

Mileage scale: 25 50 miles / 25 50 75 kilometers

SCENIC TRAIL

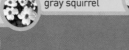

NORTH CAROLINA

The Tar Heel STATE

Bordered by the misty Blue Ridge Mountains to the west and miles of Atlantic Ocean beaches to the east, North Carolina is a state of towering turf and pristine surf. In between lie old tobacco plantations, high-tech cities, and detours to America's past. The state's nickname comes from North Carolina's long history of producing tar from local pine forests.

Highest point in North Carolina and east of the Mississippi

TRAFFIC LAWS
YOU WON'T BELIEVE

It's illegal to drive a car equipped with a smoke screen device.

It is forbidden to hurl rocks at the roads in Dunn.

Rollerblading on state highways isn't just a bad idea—it's illegal in Southern Shores.

GPS BOREDOM BUSTER!
Plot a course along the Blue Ridge Parkway using your GPS. Stop at the scenic overlooks to snap postcard-worthy pics!

Roadside Attractions

TEACH'S HOLE
Learn all about the bloodthirsty pirate Blackbeard, aka Edward Teach, whose buccaneering career came to a gruesome end off Ocracoke Island.

GIGANTIC DRESSER
The four-story chest of drawers in High Point even has a pair of gigantic dangling socks. Better hope they're not stinky!

THE BLOWING ROCK
Snow has been known to blow upside down at this 4,000-foot (1.2-km) cliff near the town of the same name.

5 COOL THINGS TO DO HERE

1 BLUE RIDGE PARKWAY
Cherokee

Buckle up for a hilly, curvy, topsy-turvy drive through the spectacular Appalachian Mountains.

2 SEA TURTLES
Cape Hatteras National Seashore

Watch endangered sea turtles bury their eggs on the sandy beaches of the Outer Banks, a chain of barrier islands rich in wildlife and pirate lore.

3 BILTMORE ESTATE
Asheville

Explore this amazing mansion and imagine living in a house with 65 fireplaces and a basement swimming pool.

4 MOUNT MITCHELL
Near Burnsville

Peer down upon the clouds from atop the tallest peak east of the Mississippi—more than a mile (1.6 km) high!

5 OLD SALEM
Winston-Salem

Travel back in time to a 19th-century town, where you will find costumed actors reenacting daily life in America's early years.

5 COOL THINGS TO DO HERE

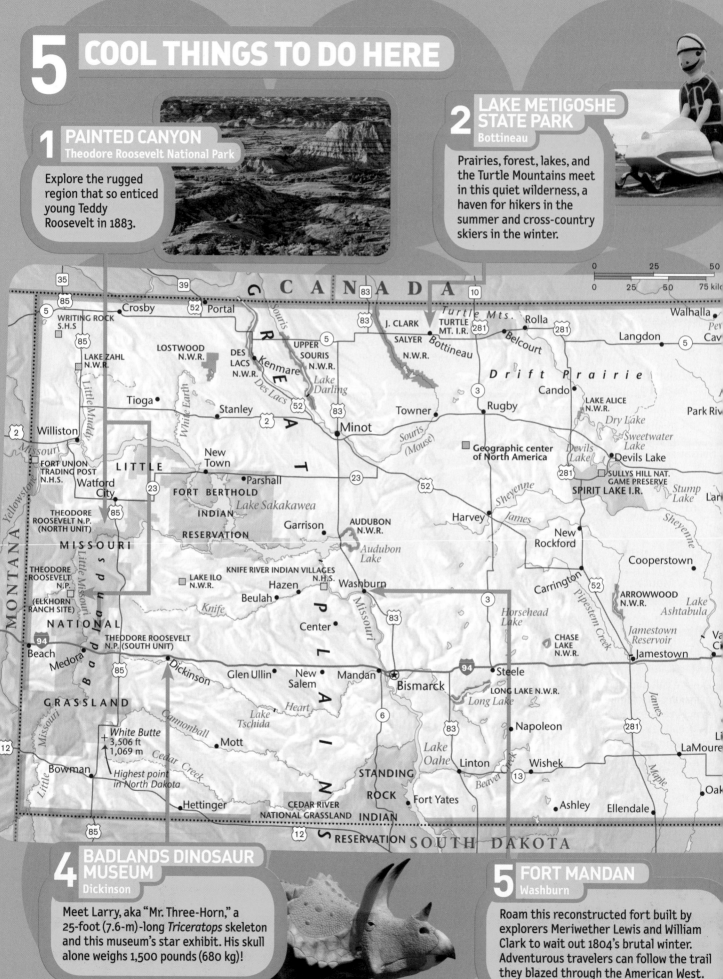

1 PAINTED CANYON
Theodore Roosevelt National Park

Explore the rugged region that so enticed young Teddy Roosevelt in 1883.

2 LAKE METIGOSHE STATE PARK
Bottineau

Prairies, forest, lakes, and the Turtle Mountains meet in this quiet wilderness, a haven for hikers in the summer and cross-country skiers in the winter.

4 BADLANDS DINOSAUR MUSEUM
Dickinson

Meet Larry, aka "Mr. Three-Horn," a 25-foot (7.6-m)-long *Triceratops* skeleton and this museum's star exhibit. His skull alone weighs 1,500 pounds (680 kg)!

5 FORT MANDAN
Washburn

Roam this reconstructed fort built by explorers Meriwether Lewis and William Clark to wait out 1804's brutal winter. Adventurous travelers can follow the trail they blazed through the American West.

STATE BIRD:
western meadowlark

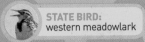
STATE FLOWER:
wild prairie rose

STATE TREE:
American elm

STATE CAPITAL: Bismarck
AREA: 70,700 sq mi (183,113 sq km)

NORTH DAKOTA

The Roughrider STATE

3 BONANZAVILLE
West Fargo

Tour the schoolhouses, workshops—even the jail—of an authentic pioneer village.

I f the grain silos, ghost towns, and endless wheat fields of eastern North Dakota don't sound like sights you need to see, then go west, young road-tripper! You'll find the bison-filled badlands that made a man out of Theodore Roosevelt, America's most rough-and-tumble president.

FANTASTIC NORTH DAKOTA FACTS

You can walk to Canada and back inside the Peace Chapel at the International Peace Garden on the border of North Dakota and Manitoba, Canada.

Farms and ranches cover 90 percent of North Dakota.

When three outlaws stole Teddy Roosevelt's boat on the Missouri River in 1886, he built a new one and chased down the thieves!

BOREDOM BUSTER!
Take a photo of every ghost town you pass and see how many you can find!

Roadside Attractions

ENCHANTED HIGHWAY
Artist Gary Greff decorated this 32-mile (51-km) stretch of roadway east of Dickinson with scrap metal sculptures of bugs, birds, and fanciful beasts.

WORLD'S LARGEST BUFFALO
Herds of buffalo roam the state's badlands, but none are as large as this buffalo statue. It stands 26 feet (7.9 m) tall near Jamestown, North Dakota's "Buffalo City."

A ROCKIN' MUSEUM
The Paul Broste Rock Museum in Parshall houses the largest rock collection in the state. Check out geodes, opals, and even a dinosaur egg!

Map labels: bina, 29, rand orks, wood, le, sboro, MINNESOTA, Red River of the North, ton, Fargo, West Fargo, 29, Sheyenne, SHEYENNE NATIONAL GRASSLAND, Wahpeton, 13, Wild Rice, TEWAUKON N.W.R., Hankinson, 29, LAKE TRAVERSE (SISSETON) INDIAN RESERVATION

Travel from one end of Ohio to the other and you'll have a tough time believing you're still in the same state. Factories along the Ohio River give way to forests in the south, while horse-drawn buggies outnumber automobiles in the quaint Amish communities of the state's heart.

TRAFFIC LAWS
YOU WON'T BELIEVE

If you want to roller-skate on the street in Canton, you better ask the police first.

It might sound like common sense, but you're not allowed to ride on the roof of a taxi in Youngstown.

You can't ride a horse on the sidewalk in Marietta.

OHIO
The Buckeye STATE

STATE BIRD: cardinal

STATE FLOWER: red carnation

STATE ANIMAL: white-tailed deer

STATE CAPITAL: Columbus

AREA: 44,825 sq mi (116,097 sq km)

Roadside Attractions

ROCK AND ROLL HALL OF FAME
Inspect the instruments and artifacts of legendary guitar heroes at this seven-story museum on the shore of Lake Erie in Cleveland.

FIELD OF GIANT CORN COBS
With 109 sculptures of concrete corncobs, each more than six feet (1.9 m) tall, it's hard to miss this unique cornfield in Dublin.

PRO FOOTBALL HALL OF FAME
Gridiron greats score the ultimate honor at this Canton museum of the National Football League.

---

5 COOL THINGS TO DO HERE

1 STEEL BEASTS
Sandusky

Give your stomach the topsy-turvy treatment at Cedar Point, an amusement park famous for its roller coasters.

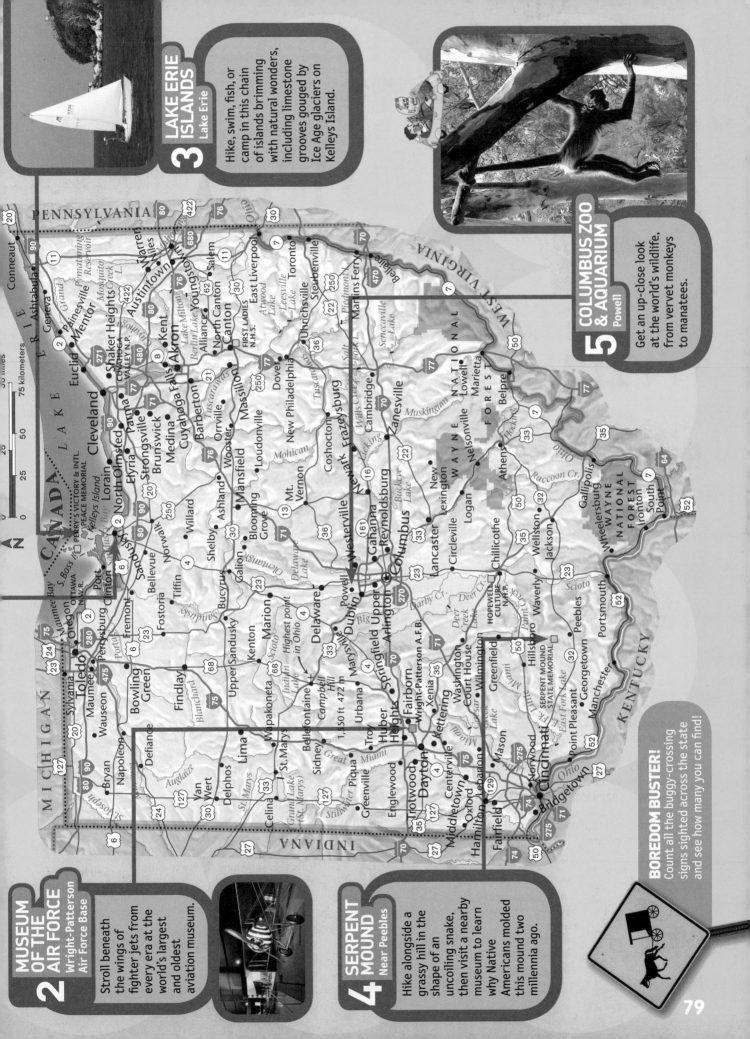

3 LAKE ERIE ISLANDS
Lake Erie

Hike, swim, fish, or camp in this chain of islands brimming with natural wonders, including limestone grooves gouged by Ice Age glaciers on Kelleys Island.

5 COLUMBUS ZOO & AQUARIUM
Powell

Get an up-close look at the world's wildlife, from vervet monkeys to manatees.

2 MUSEUM OF THE AIR FORCE
Wright-Patterson Air Force Base

Stroll beneath the wings of fighter jets from every era at the world's largest and oldest aviation museum.

4 SERPENT MOUND
Near Peebles

Hike alongside a grassy hill in the shape of an uncoiling snake, then visit a nearby museum to learn why Native Americans molded this mound two millennia ago.

BOREDOM BUSTER!
Count all the buggy-crossing signs sighted across the state and see how many you can find!

PENNSYLVANIA

WEST VIRGINIA

CANADA

LAKE ERIE

MICHIGAN

INDIANA

KENTUCKY

STATE BIRD: scissor-tailed flycatcher

STATE FLOWER: Oklahoma rose

STATE ANIMAL: buffalo

STATE CAPITAL: Oklahoma City
AREA: 69,898 sq mi (181,036 sq km)

OKLAHOMA

The Sooner STATE

From sweeping plains to diverse forests to vast grasslands, Oklahoma has a varied landscape. Besides its natural wonders, there's plenty of fun to be had here, too! This state is also in a unique location: Oklahoma is an equal distance from the East and West Coasts of the U.S.

COLORADO map
Cimarron
Black Mesa 4,973 ft 1,516 m
Kenton
Highest point in Oklahoma
Boise City
Guymon
N.M.
KIOWA AND RITA BLANCA NATIONAL GRASSLANDS
OPTIMA N.W.R.
Optima Lake
HIGH PLAINS
83 54
64
412
287
54

FANTASTIC OKLAHOMA FACTS

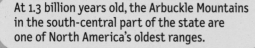

The shopping cart was invented in Oklahoma City.

At 1.3 billion years old, the Arbuckle Mountains in the south-central part of the state are one of North America's oldest ranges.

The state capitol building has a working oil rig on its grounds.

GPS BOREDOM BUSTER!
Nearly 400 miles (644 km) of historic Route 66 still stretch across Oklahoma—from Texola to Quapaw. Use your GPS and some detective work to trace the famous highway's path.

Roadside Attractions

THE BLUE WHALE
A smiling concrete sperm whale guards a swimming hole off old Route 66 near Catoosa.

WINDMILL MUSEUM & PARK
More than 50 vintage windmills—some from the 1800s—sprout from this sprawling shrine to wind power in Shattuck.

GOLDEN DRILLER
Like some fossil-fuel-powered superhero, this gold-painted oil worker looms over Tulsa as a monument to the city's days as the "oil capital of the world."

4 BLACK MESA
Kenton

Hike to the flat top of this mesa covered in black volcanic rock. Nearly 5,000 feet (1.5 km) above sea level, it's Oklahoma's highest point.

5 WICHITA MOUNTAIN WILDLIFE REFUGE
Lawton

See herds of bison, longhorn cattle, elk, and other Great Plains regulars roam this rocky region popular with climbers.

5 COOL THINGS TO DO HERE

1 OKLAHOMA ROUTE 66 MUSEUM
Clinton

Route 66, the two-lane "Main Street of America" that once linked Chicago and Los Angeles is an icon of American road-tripping. Stop by this museum to learn about the route's vibrant days before it was replaced by superhighways.

2 FRONTIER CITY
Oklahoma City

Only a bronco bucks harder than the roller coasters at this Wild West–themed amusement park.

3 CHEROKEE HERITAGE MUSEUM
Tahlequah

The Cherokee were one of many Native American tribes forced to resettle in Oklahoma in the early 1800s. See demonstrations of Native American games and weapons at this re-creation of a 17th-century village.

81

OREGON

The Beaver STATE

1 MOUNT HOOD
Mount Hood National Forest

The snowcapped peak of Oregon's tallest mountain makes a stunning backdrop for hiking, camping, and mountain biking.

Promises of wide-open land and the good life lured enterprising pioneers west along the roughly 2,000-mile (3,200-km) Oregon Trail in the 1840s. Not much has changed! Today's visitors to Oregon find an incredible variety of landscapes and sophisticated cities offering every type of attraction.

Roadside Attractions

GILBERT HOUSE CHILDREN'S MUSEUM

The biggest attraction of this interactive museum in Salem is its sprawling backyard playground, featuring a gigantic Erector set, a miniature village, a woolly mammoth dig site, and lots of other stuff to climb on.

EVERGREEN AVIATION & SPACE MUSEUM

This hangar in McMinnville is home to more than 200 aircraft—including the *Spruce Goose,* one of the largest planes ever built!

VACUUM MUSEUM

The shelves of Stark's Vacuums store in Portland are lined with hundreds of dirt-devouring contraptions from throughout housecleaning history. One model requires two people to operate!

TRAFFIC LAWS
YOU WON'T BELIEVE

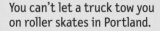

Don't leave your car door open longer than you have to—it's a crime!

You can't let a truck tow you on roller skates in Portland.

You're not allowed to compete in a push-up contest while driving on the highway.

BOREDOM BUSTER!
Deserts, forests, mountains, jagged coastline—Oregon's range of terrain is vast! Try to capture each environment with your camera as you travel through the state.

PACIFIC OCEAN

Ast
LEWIS & C
Seasid
CAP
MEARES
N.W.R.
Tillamo
Lincoln City
Newport
NA
101
FOR
Florence
Reed
OREGON DUNES
N.R.A.
Unt
COOS, LOWER, UMPQUA, AND SUISLAW I.R.
North
Coos Bay
Coos Bay
COQUILL
I.R.
BANDON
MARSH
N.W.R.
Coqui
101
Cape Blanco
SISKIYOU
Gold Beach
Rogu
NATION
Brookings
F
101

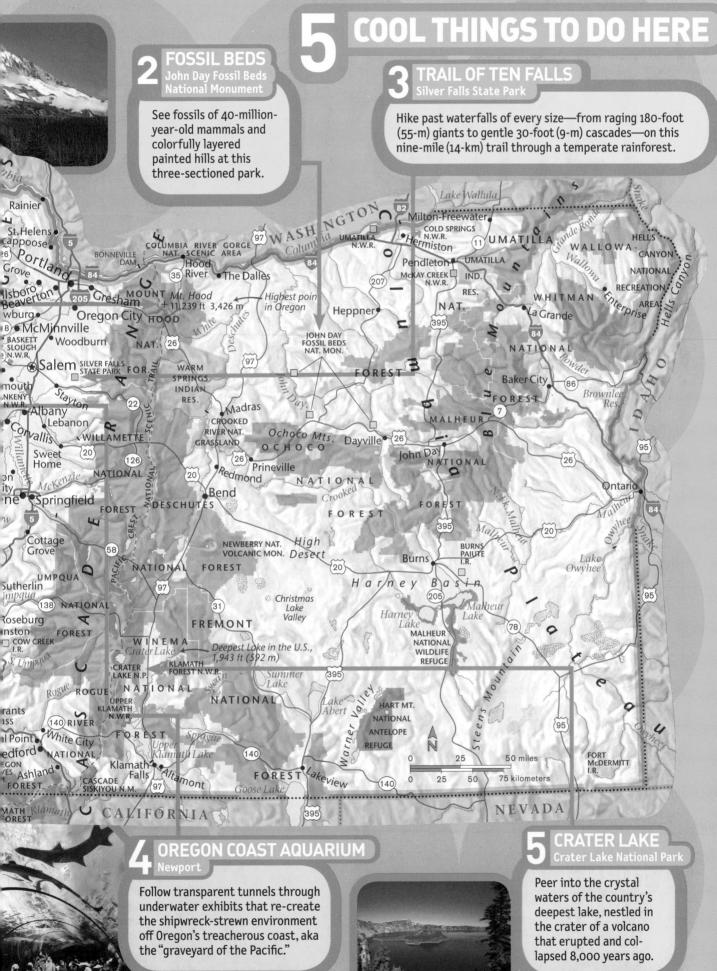

5 COOL THINGS TO DO HERE

2 FOSSIL BEDS
John Day Fossil Beds National Monument

See fossils of 40-million-year-old mammals and colorfully layered painted hills at this three-sectioned park.

3 TRAIL OF TEN FALLS
Silver Falls State Park

Hike past waterfalls of every size—from raging 180-foot (55-m) giants to gentle 30-foot (9-m) cascades—on this nine-mile (14-km) trail through a temperate rainforest.

4 OREGON COAST AQUARIUM
Newport

Follow transparent tunnels through underwater exhibits that re-create the shipwreck-strewn environment off Oregon's treacherous coast, aka the "graveyard of the Pacific."

5 CRATER LAKE
Crater Lake National Park

Peer into the crystal waters of the country's deepest lake, nestled in the crater of a volcano that erupted and collapsed 8,000 years ago.

PENNSYLVANIA

The Keystone STATE

0   25   50 miles
0   25   50   75 kilometers

Map labels: LAKE ERIE, Erie, Millcreek, 90, 20, OHIO, 6N, 79, Meadville, ERIE NAT WIL REF, Pymatuning Reservoir, 322, Greenville, 62, Sharon, 80, New Castle, Grove City, 422, 376, 422, 76, Beaver Falls, Tarer, B, 30, McCandless, Aliquippa, Ohio, 279, Pittsburgh, 22, 376, McKeesport, Avella, 79, 43, 51, Washington, Monessen, 70, 40, 79, Union Farmi, Waynesburg, Monongahela, Laurel Cavern, 119, WEST VIRGINIA

Talk about a state with a history! America's founding principles were drafted in Philadelphia, but Pennsylvania's story goes back another 16,000 years to the oldest known human shelter in North America. What's made the Keystone State such a hot spot since the Ice Age? Hit the turnpike and find out!

FANTASTIC PENNSYLVANIA FACTS

The banana split was created in 1904 in Latrobe by a 23-year-old man.

The state is known for its handmade pretzels and whoopie pies.

The first zoo in the U.S. was in Philadelphia.

▼ Roadside Attractions

MÜTTER MUSEUM
You don't have to be a medical student to visit this collection of anatomical oddities—from human skulls to barbaric surgical instruments—in Philadelphia.

THE CRAYOLA FACTORY
See how Crayola crayons and markers are made and then color and create to your heart's desire at this cool and colorful visitor center in Easton.

KAVERNPUTT
This 18-hole mini-golf course in Farmington is set inside a creepy artificial cave right next to Laurel Caverns, Pennsylvania's largest real cave.

3 ROBOWORLD
Pittsburgh

Get inside the mechanical minds of the world's smartest robots—and even challenge one to a basketball game—at the Carnegie Science Center.

PENNA TURN-PIKE

GPS BOREDOM BUSTER!
The Pennsylvania Turnpike was America's first superhighway. Use your GPS to track all the major cities linked by this famous route.

5 COOL THINGS TO DO HERE

1 MEADOWCROFT ROCKSHELTER
Avella

Try wielding the primitive tools and weapons of prehistoric people who used this mountain cave as a campsite 16,000 years ago.

2 INDEPENDENCE HALL
Philadelphia

Visit the chamber where America's Founding Fathers signed the Declaration of Independence and the U.S. Constitution, just across the street from the Liberty Bell.

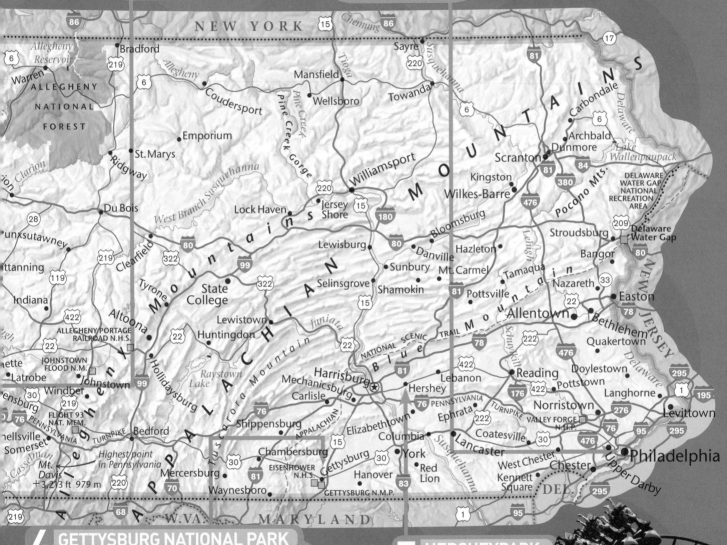

4 GETTYSBURG NATIONAL PARK
Gettysburg

Tour the farm fields where Union troops of the north narrowly won a crucial battle against the southern Confederacy during the Civil War.

5 HERSHEYPARK
Hershey

Experience a sugar rush and an adrenaline rush at this theme park in Hershey, home of the famous chocolate company.

STATE BIRD: Rhode Island red chicken

STATE FLOWER: violet

STATE TREE: red maple

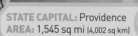
STATE CAPITAL: Providence
AREA: 1,545 sq mi (4,002 sq km)

RHODE ISLAND

The Ocean STATE

t may be the nation's tiniest state—just over half the size of the second smallest, Delaware—but Rhode Island delivers big on sights worth seeing. White-sand beaches, lush woodlands, and countless historic landmarks fill an area smaller than some American cities.

Roadside Attractions

FLYING HORSE CAROUSEL
In Watch Hill, take a spin on the hand-carved wooden horses of the oldest carousel of its kind in the country.

BIG BLUE BUG
Watch out for the titanic termite looming over Interstate 95 in Providence! (It's actually the famous fiberglass mascot of a pest-control company.)

THE BREAKERS MANSION
Admire the crystal chandeliers, marble walls, and stunning Atlantic views of this 70-room Newport summer home modeled after a 16th-century palace.

TRAFFIC LAWS
YOU WON'T BELIEVE

It's against the law to race horses on the highway.

It's illegal to string a wire that is less than 14 feet (4.3 m) high across a roadway.

Never pass a car on the left without honking your horn first.

GPS BOREDOM BUSTER!
Use your GPS to see how long it would take to drive through Rhode Island. Compare it to a trip across Alaska, the largest state.

5 COOL THINGS TO DO HERE

1 ROGER WILLIAMS PARK ZOO
Providence

Watch snow leopards prowl and otters waddle and swim at one of the nation's oldest zoos.

2 SCHOONER SAIL
Newport

Sail Narragansett Bay in 19th-century style aboard the passenger yachts that depart from Newport.

3 FORT ADAMS
Newport

Patrol the bastions and explore the tunnels of the largest coastal fortification in America, built to protect Narragansett Bay in the 1800s.

4 LIGHTHOUSE KEEPER
Rose Island

Don't visit this lighthouse inn expecting a good night's sleep. It's your job to operate the beacon just like it was done back in 1912!

5 BLOCK ISLAND
Block Island

Hop a ferry to this quaint island and spend the day hiking, bird-watching, or just sunbathing on a quiet beach.

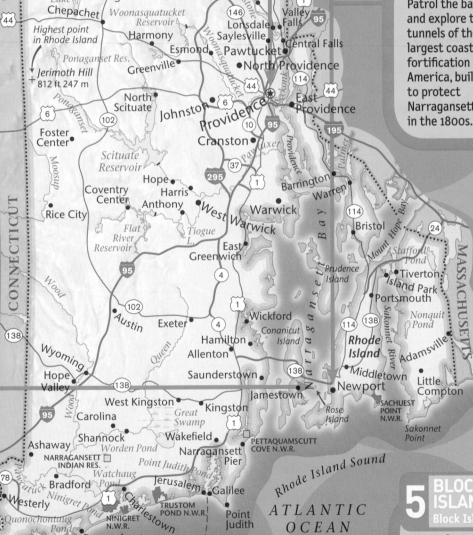

MASSACHUSETTS

Woonsocket

Slatersville · Glendale · Harrisville · Pascoag · Chepachet

Wallum Lake · Pascoag Lake

Union Village · Manville · Cumberland Hill · Ashton · Valley Falls · Lonsdale · Saylesville · Central Falls

Pawtucket Reservoir

Blackstone

Highest point in Rhode Island
Jerimoth Hill
812 ft 247 m

Harmony · Esmond · Pawtucket · North Providence

Woonasquatucket Reservoir

Ponaganset Res.

Greenville

North Scituate · Johnston · Providence · East Providence

CONNECTICUT

Foster Center

Scituate Reservoir

Cranston

Hope · Harris · Anthony

Coventry Center

Rice City

Flat River Reservoir

Tiogue L.

West Warwick · Warwick

Barrington · Warren · Bristol

Mount Hope Bay

Stafford Pond

Tiverton · Island Park · Portsmouth

MASSACHUSETTS

East Greenwich

Wickham · Conanicut Island · Prudence Island

Austin · Exeter

Hamilton · Allenton

Saunderstown

Nonquit Pond

Rhode Island

Adamsville

Middletown · Newport

Little Compton

Wyoming · Hope Valley

Jamestown

West Kingston · Kingston

Carolina · Shannock · Wakefield

Great Swamp

Rose Island

SACHUEST POINT N.W.R.

Sakonnet Point

Ashaway · Bradford

NARRAGANSETT INDIAN RES.

Watchaug Pond · Worden Pond

Narragansett Pier

PETTAQUAMSCUTT COVE N.W.R.

Westerly · Jerusalem · Galilee

Rhode Island Sound

Ninigret Pond · Charlestown · Point Judith

TRUSTOM POND N.W.R.

ATLANTIC OCEAN

Quonochontaug Pond

NINIGRET N.W.R.

Quonochontaug

Watch Hill

N.Y.

Napatree Point

Block Island Sound

Sandy Point

BLOCK ISLAND N.W.R.

Block Island

Block Island

0   5   10 miles
0   5   10   15 kilometers

STATE BIRD: Carolina wren

STATE FLOWER: yellow jessamine

STATE ANIMAL: white-tailed deer

STATE CAPITAL: Columbia
AREA: 32,020 sq mi (82,932 sq km)

SOUTH CAROLINA

The Palmetto STATE

South Carolina is a state for every sort of buff. Blackbeard buffs come to learn about the pirate king's 1718 blockade of Charleston. Civil War buffs climb the walls of Fort Sumter, unchanged since the war's first battle. Beach buffs frolic on Myrtle Beach's stand of golden sand. What sort of buff are you? Find out in the Palmetto State!

FANTASTIC
SOUTH CAROLINA FACTS

South Carolina was the first state to secede from the Union in the Civil War.

Built in 1735, Charleston's Dock Street Theatre is said to be one of America's most haunted buildings.

South Carolina grows more peaches than any state east of the Mississippi.

BOREDOM BUSTER!
More and more films are being shot in the Carolinas. Follow Hollywood's lead and use your camera to make a movie of your South Carolina vacation!

Roadside Attractions

MIDDLETON PLACE
Footpaths meander around a butterfly-shaped lake and beneath dangling Spanish moss at this old Charleston plantation once described as the "premier garden of the 13 Colonies."

MINI-GOLF CAPITAL OF THE WORLD
Putt-Putt pros could spend a lifetime in Myrtle Beach, home to 50 miniature golf courses fitting every theme, from Jurassic lizards to scurvy pirates.

WORLD'S LARGEST PEACH
Standing four stories tall alongside Interstate 85 in Gaffney, this tasty-looking peach—actually a water tower—is a monument to the state's juiciest crop.

5 COOL THINGS TO DO HERE

1 CAROWINDS
Fort Mill

Choose from 13 roller coasters or take a dip in Tidal Wave Bay at this amusement park on the border between North and South Carolina.

2 BARRED OWLS
Congaree National Park

Listen for haunting hoots during evening "owl prowls" led by rangers in this flooded forest.

3 FORT SUMTER
Charleston

Explore the battlements of this island fortress that came under Confederate attack in 1861, the first salvos of the Civil War.

4 WORLD'S BIGGEST BOY
Columbia

It takes guts as well as brains to be a 40-foot (12-m)-tall kid. See for yourself when you climb into the head and slide out the intestines of Eddie, the centerpiece of Columbia's EdVenture children's museum.

5 HUNTING ISLAND
Hunting Island State Park

Wander beaches and lagoons empty of people but crowded with loggerhead turtles, alligators, dolphins—even the occasional seahorse!

NORTH CAROLINA

GEORGIA

ATLANTIC OCEAN

Long Bay

0   25   50 miles
0   25   50   75 kilometers

COWPENS N.B.
Highest point in South Carolina
KINGS MOUNTAIN N.M.P.
Gaffney
Greer
Taylors
Mauldin
Simpsonville
Spartanburg
York
Rock Hill
Fort Mill
Lake Wylie
Belton
Laurens
Clinton
Union
SUMTER NATIONAL FOREST
Lancaster
Cheraw
Bennettsville
Winnsboro
Hartsville
Dillon
Greenwood
Newberry
Camden
Darlington
Mullins
Abbeville
NINETY SIX N.H.S.
Lake Murray
Irmo
Florence
Marion
Loris
SUMTER NATIONAL FOREST
J. Strom Thurmond Reservoir
West Columbia
Cayce
Forest Acres
Columbia
Sumter
Conway
North Myrtle Beach
Batesburg-Leesville
Edgefield
Manning
Kingstree
Myrtle Beach
Socastee
Surfside Beach
North Augusta
Aiken
Clearwater
Williston
Bamberg
Orangeburg
SANTEE N.W.R.
Santee Dam
Black
Georgetown
Garden City
Barnwell
Lake Marion
Lake Moultrie
FRANCIS MARION NATIONAL FOREST
ATLANTIC
North Island
OCEAN
Allendale
Summerville
Walterboro
Ladson
Goose Creek
Hanahan
Moncks Corner
CAPE ROMAIN N.W.R.
Cape Island
Hampton
North Charleston
CHARLES PINCKNEY N.H.S.
Mt. Pleasant
FT. SUMTER N.M.S.
ACE BASIN N.W.R.
Charleston
Burton
Beaufort
Edisto Island
St. Helena Sound
Port Royal
HUNTING ISLAND S.P.
PINCKNEY ISLAND N.W.R.
SAVANNAH N.W.R.
Hilton Head Island
Hilton Head Island
Daufuskie Island
Port Royal Sound
St. Helena Island
Parris Island
CONGAREE NATIONAL PARK

SOUTH DAKOTA

The Mount Rushmore STATE

South Dakota may be home to America's biggest rock stars—the dynamite-sculpted presidential noggins of Mount Rushmore—but don't limit your visit to just this Black Hills attraction. Otherworldly landscapes and an enduring Native American heritage make this Great Plains state a fascinating place to explore.

FANTASTIC SOUTH DAKOTA FACTS

More than 90 percent of Mount Rushmore was carved using TNT.

Sculptors are in the process of carving Crazy Horse atop his steed at his mountainside memorial, which will be the world's largest sculpture when finished.

More than 78,000 Native Americans—one of the nation's largest populations—live in South Dakota.

GPS BOREDOM BUSTER!
Use your GPS to see how many buffalo ranches you can find, then take photos of the big furry beasts!

Roadside Attractions

THE MAMMOTH SITE
Built over a dried-up pond in Hot Springs, this enclosed research facility has unearthed the bones of more than 50 Ice Age woolly mammoths. Visitors can watch paleontologists make new discoveries daily!

WALL DRUG
What started as a tiny drugstore in the town of Wall is now a full-fledged mall famous for its Wild West souvenirs and mini Mount Rushmore.

MINUTEMAN MISSILE SITE
A holdover from America's Cold War with the Soviet Union, this remote launch facility near Wall has turned its intercontinental ballistic missile site into a tourist attraction.

1 MOUNT RUSHMORE
Black Hills

Stand face to 60-foot (18-m) face with exalted presidents George Washington, Thomas Jefferson, Theodore Roosevelt, and Abraham Lincoln at this "shrine of democracy."

3 THE BADLANDS
Badlands National Park

You'll think you landed on the surface of the moon when you visit this desolate, wind-worn landscape.

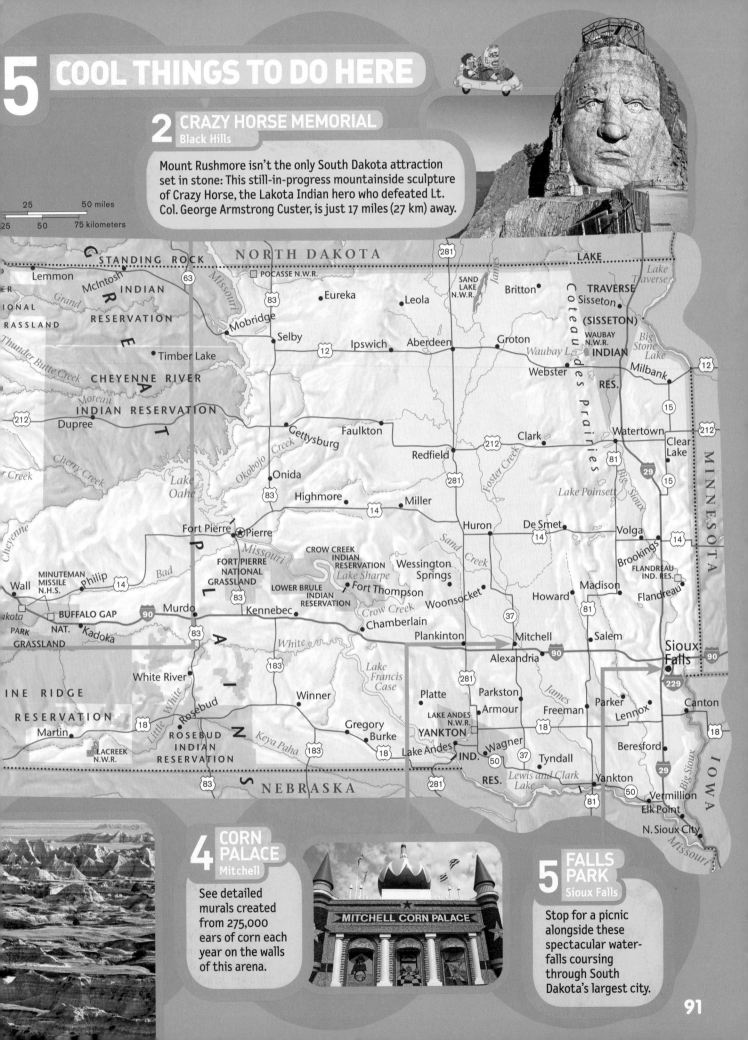

5 COOL THINGS TO DO HERE

2 CRAZY HORSE MEMORIAL
Black Hills

Mount Rushmore isn't the only South Dakota attraction set in stone: This still-in-progress mountainside sculpture of Crazy Horse, the Lakota Indian hero who defeated Lt. Col. George Armstrong Custer, is just 17 miles (27 km) away.

4 CORN PALACE
Mitchell

See detailed murals created from 275,000 ears of corn each year on the walls of this arena.

5 FALLS PARK
Sioux Falls

Stop for a picnic alongside these spectacular waterfalls coursing through South Dakota's largest city.

 **STATE BIRD:** mockingbird

 **STATE FLOWER:** iris

 STATE ANIMAL: raccoon

 **STATE CAPITAL:** Nashville
AREA: 42,143 sq mi (109,151 sq km)

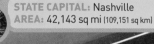

TENNESSEE

The Volunteer STATE

There's a lot to see in Tennessee—a state of misty mountains, sprawling farmland, and rolling hills—but there's even more to hear. The home of rock-and-roll and country music, Tennessee adds rhythm to any cross-country road trip.

FANTASTIC TENNESSEE FACTS

Great Smoky Mountains National Park, located in the eastern part of the state, is the most visited national park in the U.S.

Milk is the official state beverage.

An earthquake in 1812 made the Mississippi River run backward.

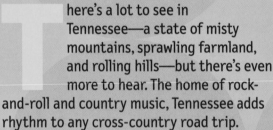

Roadside Attractions

GPS BOREDOM BUSTER!
Use your GPS to track down Elvis-themed sights as you cruise across the late superstar's home state.

DAVY CROCKETT'S BIRTHPLACE
Tennessee was still the wild frontier when folk hero Davy Crockett grew up here in the late 1700s. Stop by his Limestone birthplace and learn which of Crockett's tall tales are actually true.

DOLLYWOOD
Songstress Dolly Parton opened this country-music-themed amusement park in Pigeon Forge, complete with a roller coaster that plunges through an actual mountain.

5 COOL THINGS TO DO HERE

2 COUNTRY MUSIC HALL OF FAME
Nashville

Tap your cowboy boots to catchy tunes and learn the rich history of honky-tonk.

1 GRACELAND
Memphis

Tour the ludicrously lavish mansion of Elvis Presley, the hip-swaying king of rock-and-roll. One jungle-themed room even has its own waterfall!

3 CLINGMANS DOME
Great Smoky Mountains National Park

The grueling half-mile (0.8-km) hike to this remote observation post is worth it for the spectacular 360-degree views of the Great Smoky Mountains.

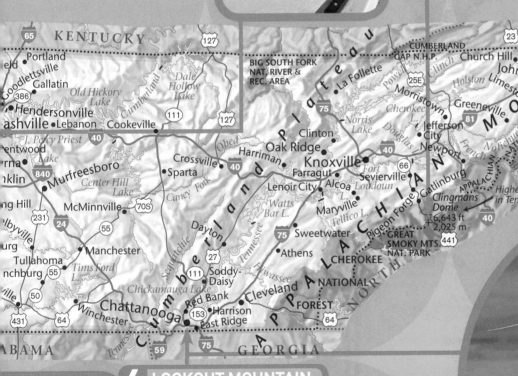

4 LOOKOUT MOUNTAIN
Chattanooga

Take a steep train ride up a mountainside for panoramic views of seven states. Then take a five-minute walk from the railway to Point Park, the site of the Civil War's "Battle Above the Clouds."

5 RIVER OTTERS
Chattanooga

Watch these rambunctious mammals play silly games at the Tennessee Aquarium, or tune in via a live web camera to see the swift swimmers from anywhere!

STATE BIRD: mockingbird
STATE FLOWER: bluebonnet
STATE ANIMAL: Texas longhorn
STATE CAPITAL: Austin
AREA: 268,581 sq mi (695,624 sq km)

TEXAS
The Lone Star STATE

1 GRAND CANYON OF TEXAS
Palo Duro Canyon State Park

Take a horseback ride through this colorful 800-foot (244-m)-deep canyon in the Texas Panhandle.

Everything isn't really bigger in Texas, despite what T-shirt slogans will tell you, but Texas is certainly big enough to hold everything. Mountains, deserts, swamps, beaches, historic towns, and vast stretches of cowboy country make up this land of unlimited adventure.

FANTASTIC TEXAS FACTS

Mission controllers in Houston were the first people on Earth to speak to the American astronauts who landed on the moon in 1969.

Texas' official state sport is rodeo.

Famous frontier adventurers Davy Crockett and James Bowie both died at the Battle of the Alamo.

BOREDOM BUSTER!
Take pictures of any oil pumps you pass and see how many you can find!

Roadside Attractions

CADILLAC RANCH
Ten graffiti-splattered Cadillacs stick up trunk-first from the sunbaked ground just west of Amarillo on Interstate 40. Planted by an eccentric millionaire in the 1970s, they've become America's most famous example of road art.

NATIONAL COWGIRL MUSEUM
This Fort Worth hall of fame features galleries and hands-on exhibits celebrating legendary women of the American West.

SCHLITTERBAHN WATERPARKS
It doesn't take long to work up a sweat in steamy Texas. Cool your heels at one of the wild Schlitterbahn Waterparks, located in Galveston, New Braunfels, and South Padre Island.

5 COOL THINGS TO DO HERE

HIGH PLAINS

KIOWA & RITA BLANCA NAT. GRASSLANDS

BLACK KETTLE N.G.

Perryton

Dumas

Borger

Pampa

LAKE MEREDITH N.R.A.

Amarillo

BUFFALO LAKE N.W.R.

Canyon

PALO DURO CANYON S.P.

Hereford

LLANO

Plainview

MULESHOE N.W.R.

Levelland

ESTACADO

Lubbock

Brownfield

Lamesa

Snyder

Andrews

Big Spring

Midland

Odessa

San Angelo

Monahans

Fort Stockton

Ozona

Sonora

2 STOCKYARDS
Fort Worth

Watch cattle drives and rodeos in the historic streets of this Fort Worth neighborhood where cowboy culture still rides high.

Childress

Vernon

Burkburnett

Wichita Falls

HAGERMAN N.W.R.

Denison

Paris

Sherman

CADDO NAT. GRASSLAND

Texarkana

ARKANSAS

Nocona

Denton

LYNDON B. JOHNSON N.G.

Mineral Wells

Breckenridge

Fort Worth

Irving

Plano

Garland

Dallas

Sulphur Springs

Mt. Pleasant

Marshall

Longview

Stephenville

Arlington

Henderson

Abilene

Corsicana

Tyler

Coleman

Brownwood

Gatesville

Waco

Palestine

Nacogdoches

SABINE NAT. FOR.

Lufkin

DAVY CROCKETT NAT. FOR.

ANGELINA NAT. FOR.

Killeen

Temple

LOUISIANA

Brady

Copperas Cove

Belton

Huntsville

Bryan

SAM HOUSTON N.F.

BIG THICKET NATIONAL PRESERVE

Georgetown

College Station

Conroe

Beaumont

LYNDON B. JOHNSON N.H.P.

Austin

Round Rock

Brenham

Kerrville

Houston

Port Arthur

McFADDIN N.W.R.

Hill Country

San Marcos

Sugar Land

Baytown

The Alamo

San Antonio

New Braunfels

Yoakum

El Campo

Galveston

AMISTAD N.R.A.

Amistad Reservoir

Del Rio

Uvalde

Victoria

Bay City

Freeport

Pearsall

Beeville

Port Lavaca

3 RIO GRANDE RAFTING
Big Bend National Park

Paddle through canyons —and conquer the occasional rapid—along the Mexico border.

Eagle Pass

Carrizo Springs

Robstown

ARANSAS N.W.R.

Rockport

Portland

Corpus Christi

Alice

Kingsville

Falfurrias

PADRE ISLAND NATIONAL SEASHORE

GULF OF MEXICO

5 SPACE CENTER
Houston

Visit Mission Control and learn what it's like to live in space at this high-tech visitor facility of the Johnson Space Center.

Laredo

Zapata

Falcon Reservoir

Rio Grande City

McAllen

LAGUNA ATASCOSA N.W.R.

South Padre I.

4 THE ALAMO
San Antonio

A famous 1836 battle at this small mission inspired Texans in their fight for independence from Mexico.

Mission

Harlingen

PALO ALTO BATTLEFIELD N.H.S.

Brownsville

Rio Grande

MEXICO

OKLAHOMA

Lake Texoma

5 COOL THINGS TO DO HERE

2 COMET BOBSLED
Park City

Rocket 80 miles an hour (129 km/h) down the actual bobsled track used in the 2002 Winter Olympic Games.

1 ZION NARROWS
Zion National Park

Hike through deep canyons of swirled sandstone at Utah's most popular park.

4 BRYCE AMPHITHEATER
Bryce Canyon

This rugged landscape's otherworldly rock spires, called hoodoos, are made of sandstone. Visit Bryce, Inspiration, Sunset, and Sunrise Points along the amphitheater for great views.

5 TRAIL OF THE ANCIENTS
Southeastern Utah

Take a road trip back in time through spectacular sandstone scenery dotted with ancestral Puebloan sites.

3 AMAZING ARCHES
Arches National Park

Eons of erosion carved this wonderland of gravity-defying sandstone bridges and precariously balanced boulders.

UTAH
The Beehive STATE

U tah has a long history as a sacred land, first to the Native Americans who built dwellings in its sandstone cliffs, and then to the Mormon pioneers who sought religious refuge near its Great Salt Lake. Today, Utah's wild range of terrain is pure heaven for outdoor enthusiasts.

FANTASTIC UTAH FACTS

In Salt Lake County, no bicycle is allowed to be equipped with a warning device such as a whistle.

It's illegal to use archery equipment to catch fish or crayfish.

Don't throw snowballs at a car (or anything else!) in Provo—it's a crime.

BOREDOM BUSTER!
Keep your eyes peeled for the rare Utah prairie dog—an endangered species—and try to capture one of these cute critters with your camera.

Roadside Attractions

HOLE IN THE ROCK
Probably the homiest cave you'll ever visit, this 14-room house—complete with a deep stone bathtub—was carved out of a massive sandstone rock near Moab.

BONNEVILLE SALT FLATS
Like the nearby Great Salt Lake, this lifeless 30,000-acre (12,140-ha) desert of salt is a remnant of an ancient inland sea. It's now a hot spot for lead-footed drivers drawn by the flats' lack of speed limits.

FANTASY CANYON
They may look like human-made sculptures, but Mother Nature gets the credit for carving the fanciful stone formations south of Vernal.

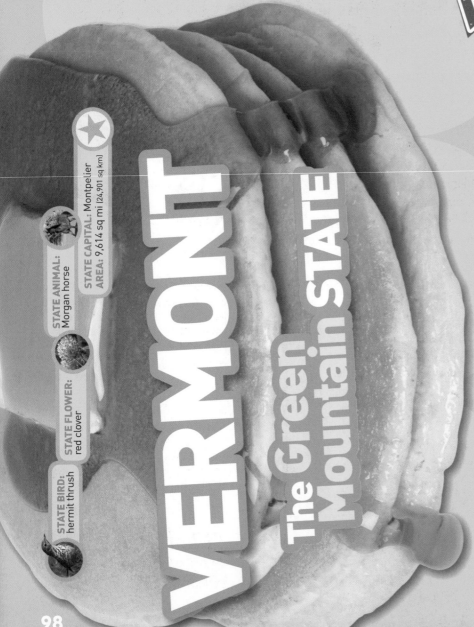

VERMONT

The Green Mountain STATE

STATE BIRD: hermit thrush

STATE FLOWER: red clover

STATE ANIMAL: Morgan horse

STATE CAPITAL: Montpelier
AREA: 9,614 sq mi (24,901 sq km)

The syrup that flows from Vermont's sugar maple trees isn't the state's sweetest attraction. Forests, mountains, and quaint villages here have remained unspoiled thanks to conservation programs and a ban on billboards. Come autumn, the countryside erupts in fall colors rivaling a fireworks finale.

FANTASTIC VERMONT FACTS

Farmers let their hogs pig out on Vermont's famous Ben & Jerry's ice cream. Mint Chocolate Cookie is the only flavor they won't eat.

Vermont produces more than a million gallons (3.8 million L) of maple syrup a year, more than any other state.

The state has more than 100,000 dairy cows.

Roadside Attractions

NEW ENGLAND MAPLE MUSEUM
Centuries ago, Native Americans discovered they could cook the sap of a maple tree to make tasty syrup. Learn the full history of Vermont's sweetest export at this Rutland museum.

SANTA'S LAND
Santa's home away from the North Pole, this whimsical village in Putney features a petting zoo with llamas, potbellied pigs, and miniature ponies.

5 COOL THINGS TO DO HERE

1 JAY PEAK
Jay
Located a few miles from the Canadian border, this resort is a powdery heaven for extreme skiers and snowboarders.

WILSON CASTLE

This 19th-century mansion in Proctor looks more like a palace than a medieval castle. Its 32 rooms, antique furnishings, and ornate stained-glass windows are certainly fit for a king.

3 SHELBURNE MUSEUM
Shelburne

Tour historic buildings and see one of the country's finest collections of folk art, tools, and other artifacts of life in colonial America.

5 NEW ENGLAND VILLAGE
Grafton

Spend a comfy night in a 200-year-old country inn in Grafton, a postcard-ready Vermont village of red barns and white-steeple churches.

GPS BOREDOM BUSTER!

Use your GPS to find some sugar-houses—small buildings that make maple syrup—and take a sweet detour to go syrup tasting!

2 LAKE CHAMPLAIN
Burlington

Take a day cruise among the rocky islands of this forest-fringed lake. Keep an eye out for Champ, Lake Champlain's version of Scotland's Loch Ness Monster!

4 FALL COLORS
Green Mountain National Forest

Vermont reveals its true colors in October, when the foliage explodes in hues from red to yellow.

20 miles
30 kilometers

N

NEW HAMPSHIRE

VERMONT

NEW YORK

MASSACHUSETTS

99

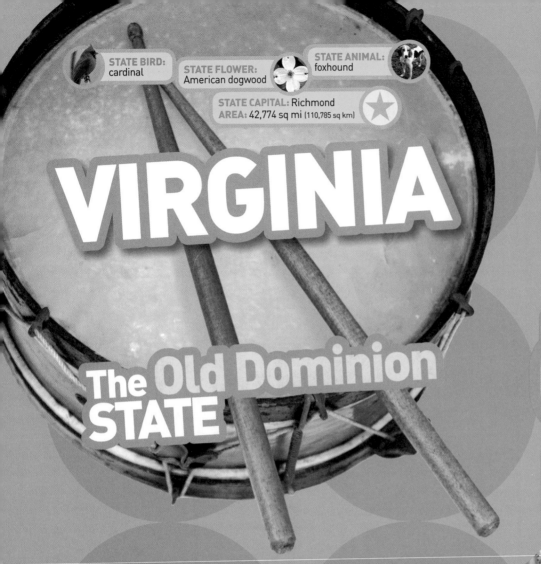

STATE BIRD: cardinal

STATE FLOWER: American dogwood

STATE ANIMAL: foxhound

STATE CAPITAL: Richmond
AREA: 42,774 sq mi (110,785 sq km)

VIRGINIA

The Old Dominion STATE

1 SKYLINE DRIVE
Shenandoah National Park

Take a dazzling road trip through the Blue Ridge Mountains, a lush sea of green in summer and a riot of reds in fall.

America's roots run deepest in Virginia, home of the first English colony and the birthplace of several Founding Fathers. But you don't have to be a history buff to appreciate the state's mountains, valleys, bays, and rivers.

FANTASTIC VIRGINIA FACTS

In 1607, Jamestown—the first English colony in what would become the U.S.—was founded in Virginia.

Eight American presidents were born in the state.

The first peanuts in the U.S. were grown in Virginia.

BOREDOM BUSTER!
Use a smartphone to research the Founding Fathers so you'll be an expert when you tour their historic haunts.

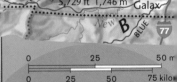

Roadside Attractions

NATURAL BRIDGE
Marvel at the natural forces that created this 20-story stone arch outside Lexington.

LURAY CAVERNS
Millions of years in the making, this subterranean wonderland in Luray is a maze of stalactites and stalagmites.

5 COOL THINGS TO DO HERE

2 MONTICELLO
Charlottesville

Thomas Jefferson wrote the Declaration of Independence, but was he any good at designing a home? See for yourself as you tour his grand residence and gardens.

3 MOUNT VERNON
Mount Vernon

Explore the mansion and 500-acre (202-ha) farm of George Washington, which has been restored to its condition during his presidency in 1789.

4 COLONIAL WILLIAMSBURG
Williamsburg

Journey back to the early days of America in this sprawling re-creation of an 18th-century city bustling with horse-drawn carriages, blacksmiths, and pedestrians in colonial clothing.

5 VIRGINIA AQUARIUM
Virginia Beach

Stand eyeball to eyeball with sharks, Komodo dragons, and crocodiles as you mosey through this vast aquarium.

STATE BIRD: goldfinch

STATE TREE: western hemlock

STATE FLOWER: coast rhododendron

STATE CAPITAL: Olympia
AREA: 71,300 sq mi (184,666 sq km)

WASHINGTON

The Evergreen STATE

0   25   50 miles
0   25   50   75 kilometers

You don't always see what you get in Washington. The famously fickle rain and fog of the Pacific Northwest can obscure attractions that lie just outside your window. Don't let a little wet weather keep you from exploring the state's spectacular mountains, rainforests, and seascapes.

FANTASTIC WASHINGTON FACTS

About 58 percent of all apples grown in the U.S. are produced in Washington. That's more than any other state.

Washington is the only state named after a U.S. president.

In 1994, 65 inches (165 cm) of snow fell at Crystal Mountain in 24 hours.

Roadside Attractions

PIKE PLACE MARKET
Not so much a roadside attraction as a Seattle institution, this lively farmers market is home to fishmongers famous for playing catch with today's catch.

MUSEUM OF GLASS
This Tacoma gallery displays delicate glass artwork from many cultures. Come see artists blow glass into fantastical shapes!

YE OLDE CURIOSITY SHOP
In business since 1899, this Seattle souvenir shop entices tourists with its gallery of oddball artifacts, including several mummies and a vampire-killer kit.

Map labels: Cape Flattery, Strait of Juan de Fuca, MAKAH I.R., OZETTE I.R., OLYMPIC COAST NATIONAL MARINE SANCTUARY, LOWER ELWHA I.R., OLYMPIC NAT. FOR., Port Ang, Olymp, 7,965 ft M, 2,428 m O, QUILEUTE I.R., Sol Duc, 101, Mountains, HOH I.R., OLYMPIC NAT. P, QUINAULT INDIAN RES., Quets, PACIFIC OCEAN, Hoquiam, Ocean Shores, Aberde, Grays Harbor, 12, SHOALWATER I.R., Willapa Bay, Raym, WILLAPA N.W.R., Cape Disappointment, JULIA BUTLE HANSEN RE, 4, 101

BOREDOM BUSTER!
The Pacific Northwest is the alleged stomping ground of Bigfoot, the mythical apelike beast. Unlike all Bigfoot photographers before you, try to capture a steady shot with your camera!

THINGS TO DO HERE

1 SPACE NEEDLE
Seattle

Take in a panoramic view of Puget Sound and the Seattle skyline from the observation deck of this famous three-legged landmark built for the 1962 World's Fair.

2 ORCAS
San Juan Islands

Watch for six-foot (1.8-m) dorsal fins slicing through the water on an orca safari around this spectacular island chain.

3 MOUNT ST. HELENS
Mount St. Helens National Volcanic Monument

See this still active volcano that blew its top—literally—in 1980, flattening more than 200 square miles (322 sq km) of surrounding forest.

4 OLYMPIC NATIONAL PARK
Olympic Peninsula

It would take a lifetime to see all of this spectacular park's snow-capped peaks, wildflower-covered meadows, waterfalls, rainforests, lakes, and rugged coastline.

5 MOUNT RAINIER
Mount Rainier National Park

Drive or hike past waterfalls and glaciers in the shadow of this snowcapped slumbering volcano.

Map Labels

CANADA

IDAHO

OREGON

Cities and Towns: Lynden, Ferndale, Bellingham, Anacortes, Sedro Woolley, Mount Vernon, Oak Harbor, Port Townsend, Everett, Snohomish, Kirkland, Redmond, Bellevue, Seattle, Renton, Burien, Federal Way, Tacoma, Auburn, Puyallup, Lakewood, Olympia, Tumwater, Centralia, Chehalis, Longview, Vancouver, Camas, Battle Ground, Omak, Republic, Colville, Wenatchee, Ephrata, Quincy, Moses Lake, Ritzville, Spokane, Medical Lake, Cheney, Pullman, Pomeroy, Clarkston, Dayton, Walla Walla, College Place, Pasco, Kennewick, Richland, Prosser, Grandview, Sunnyside, Toppenish, Yakima, Ellensburg, Connell, Othello, Goldendale

Features: Ross Lake, Okanogan National Forest, Colville National Forest, Mount Baker, North Cascades National Park, Lake Chelan N.R.A., Wenatchee National Forest, Columbia Plateau, Palouse Hills, Grand Coulee Dam, Banks Lake, Lake Roosevelt, Spokane Indian Res., Colville Indian Reservation, Kettle River Range, Pend Oreille, Kalispell I.R., Turnbull N.W.R., Columbia N.W.R., Saddle Mt. N.W.R., Hanford Reach Nat. Mon., Lake Wallula, Umatilla N.W.R., Whitman Mission N.H.S., McNary N.W.R., Blue Mountains, Umatilla National Forest, Snake River, Lake Sacajawea, Potholes Reservoir, Yakama Indian Reservation, Toppenish N.W.R., Conboy Lake N.W.R., Columbia River Gorge Nat. Scenic Area, Bonneville Dam, Gifford Pinchot National Forest, Mt. St. Helens Nat. Volcanic Mon., Mt. St. Helens 8,366 ft 2,550 m, Mount Rainier National Park, Crystal Mountain, Mt. Rainier 14,411 ft 4,392 m, Highest point in Washington, Nisqually N.W.R., Alder L., Puget Sound, San Juan Islands N.W.R., Whidbey Island, Ebey's Landing N.H.R., Cascade Range, Pacific Crest National Scenic Trail, Columbia River, Yakima River, Naches, Snake River

Rivers: Skagit, Methow, Okanogan, Sanpoil, Columbia, Spokane, Klickitat, Lewis, Cowlitz, Snake

STATE BIRD: cardinal

STATE FLOWER: rhododendron

STATE ANIMAL: black bear

STATE CAPITAL: Charleston
AREA: 24,230 sq mi (62,755 sq km)

WEST VIRGINIA

The Mountain STATE

1 COAL MINE
Beckley

Ride a mine car 1,500 feet (457 m) under a mountain to see the dirty work of old-fashioned coal mining. Not for the claustrophobic!

W est Virgina separated from Virgina and became its own state in 1863. Full of natural beauty, the state attracts outdoor enthusiasts from far and wide. With its vast forests, flowing river rapids, caves, and mountain peaks, there's no shortage of awesome adventure to be had! Coal, natural gas, and oil are some of West Virginia's natural resources.

Roadside Attractions

TRAFFIC LAWS YOU WON'T BELIEVE

It's illegal to coast down a hill with a car in neutral gear.

If you spot some tasty roadkill, you're allowed to take it home for dinner!

Bicycle riders must keep one hand on the handlebars at all times.

THE KRUGER STREET TOY & TRAIN MUSEUM
You won't find books or teachers in this old Wheeling schoolhouse, now a repository for every type of toy, from model trains to Legos.

GREENBRIER BUNKER
Once a classified underground refuge for members of Congress in the event of World War III, this decommissioned bunker in White Sulphur Springs is a fascinating monument to the Cold War.

NATIONAL RADIO ASTRONOMY OBSERVATORY
A 485-foot (147.8-m)-tall radio telescope looms above the countryside in Green Bank. Stop by to see how this observatory helps astronomers explore the universe and search for alien life.

BOREDOM BUSTER!
West Virginia is full of quaint towns. Snap a photo of each one you visit and make a map of your West Virginia road trip!

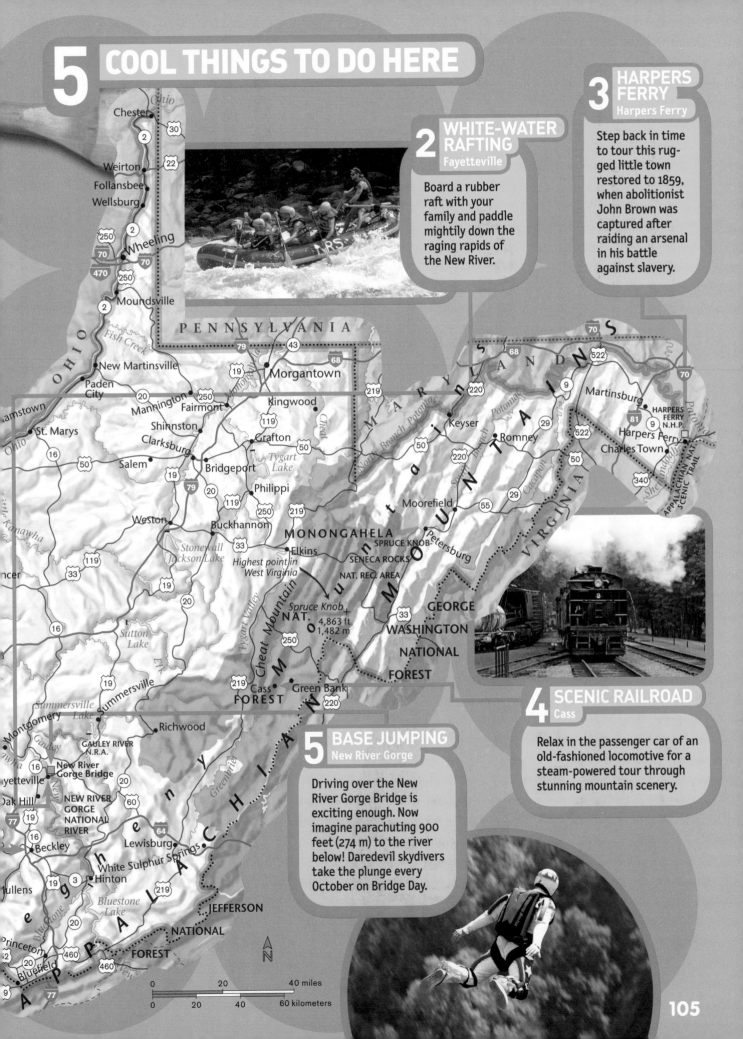

5 COOL THINGS TO DO HERE

2 WHITE-WATER RAFTING
Fayetteville

Board a rubber raft with your family and paddle mightily down the raging rapids of the New River.

3 HARPERS FERRY
Harpers Ferry

Step back in time to tour this rugged little town restored to 1859, when abolitionist John Brown was captured after raiding an arsenal in his battle against slavery.

4 SCENIC RAILROAD
Cass

Relax in the passenger car of an old-fashioned locomotive for a steam-powered tour through stunning mountain scenery.

5 BASE JUMPING
New River Gorge

Driving over the New River Gorge Bridge is exciting enough. Now imagine parachuting 900 feet (274 m) to the river below! Daredevil skydivers take the plunge every October on Bridge Day.

Map labels:

Ohio, Chester, Weirton, Follansbee, Wellsburg, Wheeling, Moundsville, New Martinsville, Paden City, St. Marys, Williamstown, Mannington, Fairmont, Shinnston, Clarksburg, Salem, Bridgeport, Philippi, Weston, Buckhannon, Spencer, Stonewall Jackson Lake, Elkins, Highest point in West Virginia, Spruce Knob 4,863 ft 1,482 m, SPRUCE KNOB, SENECA ROCKS NAT. REC. AREA, Cheat Mountain, Sutton Lake, Summersville, Summersville Lake, Richwood, Montgomery, Gauley, GAULEY RIVER N.R.A., New River Gorge Bridge, Fayetteville, Oak Hill, NEW RIVER GORGE NATIONAL RIVER, Beckley, Lewisburg, White Sulphur Springs, Mullens, Hinton, Bluestone Lake, JEFFERSON NATIONAL FOREST, Princeton, Bluefield, Kingwood, Morgantown, Grafton, Tygart Lake, Keyser, Romney, Moorefield, Petersburg, GEORGE WASHINGTON NATIONAL FOREST, Cass, FOREST, Green Bank, MONONGAHELA, MARYLAND, PENNSYLVANIA, VIRGINIA, OHIO, Martinsburg, HARPERS FERRY N.H.P., Harpers Ferry, Charles Town, APPALACHIAN NAT. SCENIC TRAIL, Potomac, North Branch Potomac, South Branch Potomac, Cacapon, Shenandoah, Fish Creek, Cheat, Little Kanawha, Elk, Greenbrier, Bluestone, Tygart Valley, MOUNTAINS, APPALACHIAN

0 20 40 miles
0 20 40 60 kilometers
N

WISCONSIN

The Badger STATE

STATE BIRD: robin

STATE ANIMAL: badger

STATE FLOWER: wood violet

STATE CAPITAL: Madison
AREA: 65,498 sq mi (169,639 sq km)

It's hardly an insult to call someone a "cheesehead" in Wisconsin, a state with so many dairy farms that "moo" is a second language. But with its thousands of lovely lakes and unspoiled state parks, Wisconsin is much more than America's cheesiest state.

FANTASTIC WISCONSIN FACTS

Green Bay is called the toilet paper capital of the world.

The French were the first Europeans to explore the area of what is now Wisconsin.

The state has more than 15,000 lakes.

Roadside Attractions

MARS' CHEESE CASTLE
Sample Wisconsin's signature goodies at this roadside fortress in Kenosha.

HOUSE ON THE ROCK
The result of an eccentric architect's imagination run amok, this sprawling compound in Spring Green is full of fanciful creatures and even has its own carousel.

WORLD'S TALLEST BICYCLE
Over 30 feet (9 m) tall, this old-time fiberglass high wheeler greets visitors to Sparta, dubbed the "bicycling capital of the world" for its many riding trails.

5 COOL THINGS TO DO HERE

1 APOSTLE ISLANDS
Bayfield

Canoe, kayak, or sail beneath the dramatic cliffs of these island jewels in Lake Superior, the world's largest freshwater body.

BOREDOM BUSTER!
Take a picture of every cow-crossing sign you pass and see how many you can find!

2 NOAH'S ARK
Wisconsin Dells

There's never a dry moment at this huge waterpark overflowing with snaking slides, lazy rivers, and churning wave pools.

3 EAA AIRVENTURE
Oshkosh

Climb into the cockpits of stomach-flipping flight simulators and build your own airplane at this museum for experimental aircraft, home to the world's wildest annual air show.

5 DOOR COUNTY
Near Green Bay

More than two million people flock to this peninsula on Lake Michigan each year for its five state parks, 11 lighthouses, and 300 miles (480 km) of scenic shoreline.

4 CAVE OF THE MOUNDS NATIONAL NATURE LANDMARK
Blue Mounds

Venture underground to marvel at crystalized rock formations and shimmering pools in the Cave of the Mounds, then hike a trail that takes you to the ground above the cave.

STATE BIRD: meadowlark

STATE FLOWER: Indian paintbrush

STATE ANIMAL: buffalo

STATE CAPITAL: Cheyenne
AREA: 97,814 sq mi (253,337 sq km)

WYOMING

The Equality STATE

1 OLD FAITHFUL
Yellowstone National Park

Watch for Old Faithful's blasts, which happen throughout the day at the country's oldest national park. The geyser blasts steamy showers 150 feet (45 m) into the air!

0   25   50 miles
0 25 50 75 kilometers

It almost seems a crime to ride anything that isn't fueled by oats through Wyoming's wide-open prairies and rugged badlands. Throw on a Stetson hat and hop into the saddle—this state's made for cowboys and cowgirls!

Roadside Attractions

FANTASTIC WYOMING FACTS

More than half of the world's geysers are in Yellowstone.

Wyoming is nicknamed the Equality State because it pioneered the right for women to vote. It was also the first state to elect a female governor.

Although Wyoming is the ninth largest state, it's home to the fewest people!

FRONTIER DAYS OLD WEST MUSEUM
Stagecoaches, saddles, firearms, and hundreds of other Wild West artifacts await in Cheyenne.

AMES PYRAMID
Off Interstate 80 near the town of Laramie, this cryptic granite monument to two railroad tycoons rises 60 feet (18 m) above the barren landscape.

JACKALOPE SQUARE
Half-jackrabbit, half-antelope, the elusive jackalope is Wyoming's official mythological creature. Its legend began in Douglas, where jackalope sightings are frequent.

LOST SPRINGS
POP   4
ELEV   4996

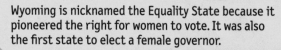

GPS BOREDOM BUSTER!
Use your GPS to find Lost Springs, one of the smallest towns in Wyoming. It has only four residents!

3 GRAND TETONS
Grand Teton National Park

Hike beneath these dramatically jagged peaks, the youngest of the Rocky Mountains.

5 COOL THINGS TO DO HERE

2 DEVILS TOWER
Northeastern Wyoming

Marvel at this unearthly stub of volcanic rock rising 1,267 feet (386 m) above the Belle Fourche River.

4 CODY NIGHT RODEO
Cody

Watch cowboys cling to bucking bulls at this nightly summer rodeo. Can't make the show? Gallop to the nearby Buffalo Bill Center of the West instead.

5 DINOSAUR DIG
Thermopolis

Spend a day helping paleontologists dig Jurassic giants out of the Bighorn Basin at the Wyoming Dinosaur Center.

CAR TRIP FUN!

TRY THESE BOREDOM-BUSTING GAMES AND ACTIVITIES ON YOUR NEXT FAMILY ROAD TRIP (OR EVEN ON A RIDE TO THE STORE).

SCAVENGER HUNT

Race your family! See who is the fastest to spot these items from the car windows.

AMERICAN FLAG

BICYCLE

BABY ON BOARD SIGN

CROPS

HAY

RAINBOW

DOG

BILLBOARD

BRIDGE

FLOCK OF BIRDS

BARN

COW

MOTORCYCLE

HORSE

GAS STATION

CAMPER

110

Undersea Stars

This underwater band is jamming onstage, but it looks as if their instruments have disappeared. Or have they? Find the 10 instruments listed below hidden in the scene.

ANSWERS ON PAGE 134

1. piano
2. drums
3. flute
4. saxophone
5. triangle
6. violin
7. accordion
8. guitar
9. maracas
10. tambourine

What in the World?

BEST OF THE NORTHWEST

These photos show close-up views of things in the Pacific Northwest. Unscramble the letters to identify what's in each picture.

ANSWERS ON PAGE 134

THE PACIFIC NORTHWEST

DEORWDO RSETE

ASCPE EDENLE

ASE TORET

EDR CORK BACR

MOTTE EOPL

ELKP TFRESO

ONTUM DOHO

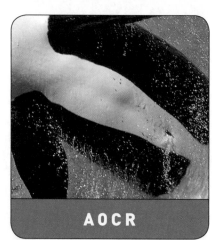

AOCR

SAELAPEN

LICENSE PLATE PUZZLER

These 51 license plates represent each state plus the District of Columbia, and together they spell out an important section of a famous American document. Identify the document by reading this puzzler.

ANSWERS ON PAGE 134

Hidden Hike

These hikers are spending St. Patrick's Day exploring the outdoors. But their adventure includes some seriously strange sights. Find at least 15 things that are wrong in the scene.

ANSWERS ON PAGE 134

What in the World?

BACKYARD BBQ

These photographs show close-up views of items you often see at a summer barbecue. Unscramble the letters to identify what's in each picture.

ANSWERS ON PAGE 135

THO ODG

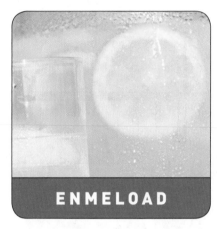

ENMELOAD

RLLIG

ATTOOP HPISC

ELONATEWRM

OKSFR

SELPTA

ADKBE EBSAN

HPETUCK

Riddle Me This

Can you answer these riddles? Read the questions on the right, then find their corresponding punch lines illustrated and marked with yellow dots throughout this museum scene. The first one has been done for you.

ANSWERS ON PAGE 135

1. What kind of shoes do spies wear?
   Sneak-ers

2. What's black and white and pink all over?

3. What has bark but no bite?

4. What comes down but never goes up?

5. What's tall when it's young and short when it's old?

6. The more you take of these, the more you leave behind.

7. What has a face and two hands but no arms or legs?

8. What can honk without a horn?

9. What has a neck but no head?

10. What invention lets you look right through a wall?

What in the World?

PURPLE PIZZAZZ

These photographs show close-up views of things that are purple. Unscramble the letters to identify what's in each picture.

ANSWERS ON PAGE 135

ISAYD

MULSP

ANRY

TGRETIL

EPGLTNGA

RSMOMOUH

EILHYJSLF

LOTLAUCCRA

HAMTTYES

117

Movie Madness

It's chaos on this crazy movie set in Hollywood. Eleven things beginning with the letter c have gone missing. Can you find the missing items in the scene so the show can go on?

ANSWERS ON PAGE 135

What in the World?

SEE WHAT YOU SEA

These photographs show close-up views of things you might see in or near the ocean. Unscramble the letters to identify what's in each picture.

ANSWERS ON PAGE 136

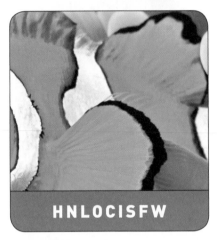

HNLOCISFW

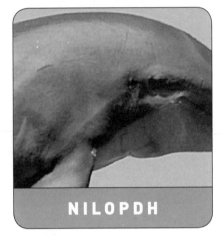

NILOPDH

NEPSSGO

FIEL TKCJESA

ASE ARTS

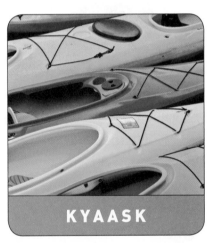

KYAASK

YLFAE ESA ONRADG

ILEF NGIR

SACLEIPN

Fishy Business

Gil and his family are going on vacation. But first he has to run some errands. Find the route that gets him from his home to the entrances of the places on his list in order. He can't swim along the same path twice and can't pass the park or the bank's door.

ANSWERS ON PAGE 136

ANSWERS ON PAGE 136

TO DO:
1. RETURN BOOK TO LIBRARY
2. BUY SWIMSUIT AT MALL
3. PICK UP SUNSCREEN AT CONVENIENCE STORE
4. GET HAIRCUT
5. CATCH SUB

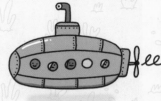

What in the World?

STEP RIGHT UP

These photos show close-up views of things you might see at a county fair. Unscramble the letters to identify what's in each picture.

ANSWERS ON PAGE 136

PGESLTI

NTTE

ZPERI NBIROB

FSRIOWKRE

CTONTO NDCYA

TKSETCI

ULNFNE ACEK

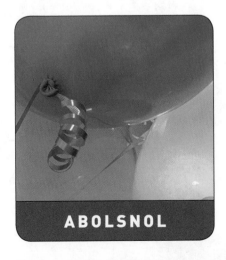

ABOLSNOL

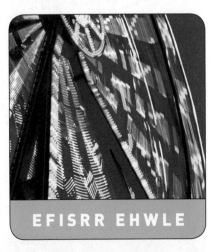

EFISRR EHWLE

City Gone Wild!

Wild animals have moved into the big city, and they're fitting in a little too well. Find the 10 wild animals hiding in this scene. Look carefully—you might see them in some funny places. ANSWERS ON PAGE 136

SIGNS
OF THE TIMES

Seeing isn't always believing. Two of these funny signs are not real. Can you figure out which two are fake?

ANSWERS ON PAGE 137

1
CAUTION CROSSING

2
AWAY FROM STRESS
HAVE A REST

3
Sand

4

5
Loch Ness Trail

6

7
NEXT BIG THING
1000 m

Go Fish!

Something's fishy at this aquarium. Find the following items that are hidden in this scene.

surfboard

cowboy hat

sunflower

wrapped gift

bike wheel

teacup and saucer

plate of spaghetti

soft pretzel

guitar

ANSWERS ON PAGE 137

What in the World?

ANSWERS ON PAGE 137

MAGIC SHOW
These photos show close-up views of magic trick props. Unscramble the letters to identify what's in each picture.

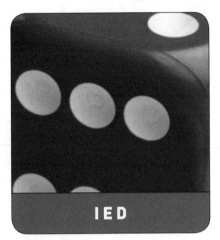

IED

KEDC FO DSRAC

KNTUR

VDOE

COKL DNA YKE

OTP ATH

EHDRIAFNCEKH

SOINC

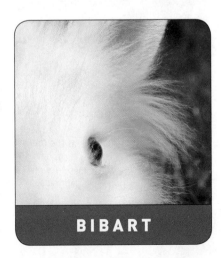

BIBART

Attention on Set

At least 10 objects at the rehearsal for *Giant Squid Versus Aliens* have the word "ten" in their names—for example, the squid's *ten*tacles. Can you spot the rest?

ANSWERS ON PAGE 137

Find the HIDDEN ANIMALS

ANIMALS OFTEN BLEND into their environments for protection. Find the animals listed below in the photographs.

ANSWERS ON PAGE 137

1. seal
2. owl
3. frog
4. lizard
5. orchid mantis

Noun Town

This city is full of nouns: people, places, and things. But 12 compound nouns—nouns made up of two or more words, or two words combined to make one word—have been drawn exactly as they're named. Can you guess the compound nouns illustrated in each of the numbered scenes? Here's a hint: The answer to number 1 is "sleeping bag."

ANSWERS ON PAGE 138

What in the World?

TRICKY TRIANGLES

These photos show close-up and faraway views of triangle shapes. Unscramble the letters to identify what's in each picture.

ANSWERS ON PAGE 138

SLAI

RVLEAETO UTNTBO

RLOTILAT HCISP

NGUEJL YMG

TJE SRTILA

RTALISWLE

UTLIQ

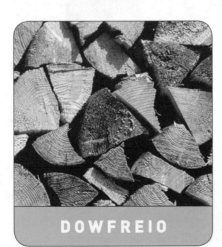

DOWFREIO

GNDUBILI

Find the HIDDEN ANIMALS

ANIMALS OFTEN BLEND
into their environments for protection. Find the animals listed below in the photographs.

ANSWERS ON PAGE 138

1. spider
2. frog
3. bald eagle
4. fox
5. jaguar
6. viscacha*

*HINT: A viscacha is a type of rodent that lives in South America.

What in the World?

BUGGING OUT!

These photographs show close-up views of creepy-crawlies. Unscramble the letters to identify what's in each picture.

ANSWERS ON PAGE 138

IRDPES

TAN

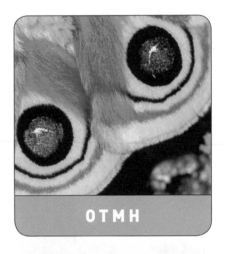

OTMH

SPAW

RNADOYFLG

RHRASGOPSEP

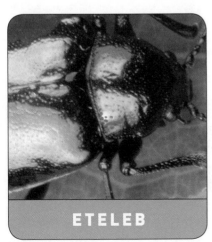

ETELEB

RACERAILPLT

ADCCAI

SIGNS
OF THE TIMES

Seeing isn't always believing. Two of these funny signs are not real. Can you figure out which two are fake?

ANSWERS ON PAGE 138

3
DUMP CLEAN DIRT HERE SEE 910

4
45 TH PARALLEL
HALFWAY BETWEEN THE EQUATOR AND THE NORTH POLE
PASS WITH CARE

5
W 37 ST

1
212 Boring

6
NO NAME ST

7
SIGN NOT IN USE

2
SURFER X-ING

8
SLIDE AREA

9
SMILE PLEASE

What in the World?

UP IN THE AIR

These photographs show close-up views of things you might see in the sky. Unscramble the letters to identify what's in each picture.

ANSWERS ON PAGE 138

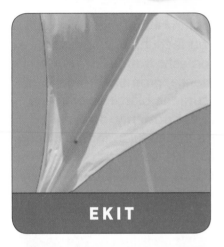

EKIT

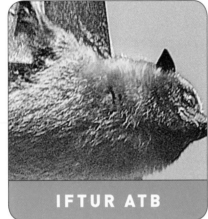

IFTUR ATB

GHAN LEDIRG

AROTPR

ECIHEPRTOL

FRIKOSWRE

RONTREHN HGTLSI

AGLYDBU

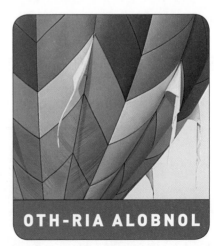

OTH-RIA ALOBNOL

ANSWERS

Undersea Stars, page 111:

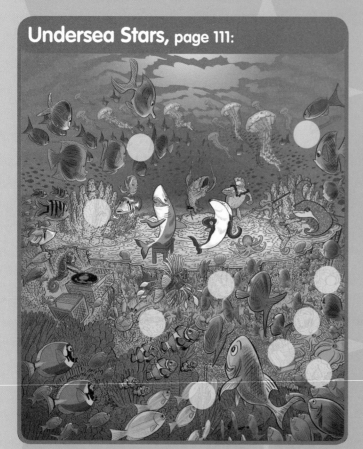

License Plate Puzzler, page 113:

We the people of the United States, in order to form a more perfect union, establish justice, insure domestic tranquility, provide for the common defense, promote the general welfare, and secure the blessings of liberty to ourselves and our posterity, do ordain and establish this Constitution for the United States of America. (These words are from the Preamble to the U.S. Constitution.)

Hidden Hike, page 114:

What in the World?
Best of the Northwest, page 112:

Top row: redwood trees, Space Needle, sea otter

Middle row: red rock crab, totem pole, kelp forest

Bottom row: Mount Hood, orca, seaplane

What in the World?
Backyard BBQ, page 115:

Top row: hot dog, lemonade, grill

Middle row: potato chips, watermelon, forks

Bottom row: plates, baked beans, ketchup

Riddle Me This, page 116:

The 10 punch lines are:
1. *sneak*-ers
2. zebra
3. tree
4. rain
5. candle
6. footsteps
7. clock
8. goose
9. bottle
10. window

What in the World?
Purple Pizzazz, page 117:

Top row: daisy, plums, yarn

Middle row: glitter, eggplant, mushroom

Bottom row: jellyfish, calculator, amethyst

Aunt Bertha appears 24 times inside this book. She's also on the cover 8 times.

Movie Madness, page 118:

The 11 things beginning with the letter *c* are:
1. car
2. cup
3. camera
4. cell phone
5. clock
6. candle
7. canary
8. coat
9. chair
10. cupcake
11. cabin

ANSWERS

What in the World?
See What You Sea, page 119:

Top row: clownfish, dolphin, sponges

Middle row: life jackets, sea star, kayaks

Bottom row: leafy sea dragon, life ring, pelicans

What in the World?
Step Right Up, page 121:

Top row: piglets, tent, prize ribbon

Middle row: fireworks, cotton candy, tickets

Bottom row: funnel cake, balloons, Ferris wheel

Fishy Business, page 120:

City Gone Wild!, page 122:

Signs of the Times, page 123:

Signs **2** and **7** are fake.

Go Fish!, page 124:

What in the World?
Magic Show, page 125:

Top row: die, deck of cards, trunk

Middle row: dove, lock and key, top hat

Bottom row: handkerchief, coins, rabbit

Attention on Set, page 126:

The 10 items with "ten" in their name are:

1. utensils
2. antenna
3. stencil
4. extension cord
5. tentacle
6. kitten
7. tent
8. Tennessee
9. tennis ball
10. mitten

Find the Hidden Animals, page 127:

1. center left
2. center right
3. top
4. bottom right
5. bottom left

ANSWERS

Noun Town, page 128:

The 12 compound nouns are:
1. sleeping bag
2. eggplant
3. catfish
4. bellhop
5. ladybug
6. housework
7. butterfly
8. limelight
9. arrowhead
10. full moon
11. sunflower
12. coffee table

What in the World?
Tricky Triangles, page 129:

Top row: sail, elevator button, tortilla chip
Middle row: jungle gym, jet trails, stairwell
Bottom row: quilt, firewood, building

Find the Hidden Animals, page 130:

1. bottom left
2. center right
3. top center
4. top right
5. bottom right
6. center left

What in the World?
Bugging Out!, page 131:

Top row: spider, ant, moth
Middle row: wasp, dragonfly, grasshopper
Bottom row: beetle, caterpillar, cicada

Signs of the Times, page 132:

Signs **5** and **8** are fake.

What in the World?
Up in the Air, page 133:

Top row: kite, fruit bat, hang glider
Middle row: parrot, helicopter, fireworks
Bottom row: northern lights, ladybug,
hot-air balloon

INDEX

Illustrations are indicated by **boldface.**

INDEX

PHOTO CREDITS

143

First edition copyright © 2012 National Geographic Society

Second edition copyright © 2020 National Geographic Partners, LLC

Published by National Geographic Partners, LLC. All rights reserved. Reproduction of the whole or any part of the contents without written permission from the publisher is prohibited.

Since 1888, the National Geographic Society has funded more than 12,000 research, exploration, and preservation projects around the world. The Society receives funds from National Geographic Partners, LLC, funded in part by your purchase. A portion of the proceeds from this book supports this vital work. To learn more, visit natgeo.com/info.

NATIONAL GEOGRAPHIC and Yellow Border Design are trademarks of the National Geographic Society, used under license.

For more information, visit nationalgeographic.com, call 1-877-873-6846, or write to the following address:

National Geographic Partners
1145 17th Street N.W.
Washington, D.C. 20036-4688 U.S.A.

Visit us online at nationalgeographic.com/books

For librarians and teachers: nationalgeographic.com/books/librarians-and-educators

More for kids from National Geographic: natgeokids.com

National Geographic Kids magazine inspires children to explore their world with fun yet educational articles on animals, science, nature, and more. Using fresh storytelling and amazing photography, *Nat Geo Kids* shows kids ages 6 to 14 the fascinating truth about the world—and why they should care.
kids.nationalgeographic.com/subscribe

For rights or permissions inquiries, please contact National Geographic Books Subsidiary Rights: bookrights@natgeo.com

Designed by Eva Absher-Schantz, Ruthie Thompson, and Kathryn Robbins

The publisher wishes to thank the book team: Priyanka Lamichhane and Libby Romero, senior editors; Julide Dengel and Callie Broaddus, art directors; Shannon Hibberd, senior photo editor; Michelle Harris, factual reviewer; Alix Inchausti, production editor; Anne LeongSon and Gus Tello, production designers

National Geographic supports K–12 educators with ELA Common Core Resources. Visit **natgeoed.org/commoncore** for more information.

The Library of Congress cataloged the 2012 edition as follows:

Boyer, Crispin.
National Geographic kids ultimate U.S. road trip atlas : maps, games, activities, and more for hours of backseat fun/by Crispin Boyer.— 1st ed.
   p. cm.
Includes bibliographical references and index.
ISBN 978-1-4263-0933-5 (pbk. : alk. paper)—
ISBN 978-1-4263-0934-2 (lib. bdg. : alk. paper)
 1. United States—Maps for children. 2. United States—Description and travel. 3. Recreation areas—United States—Maps. 4. Outdoor recreation—United States—Maps. I. Title. II. Title: Kids ultimate U.S. road trip atlas.
 G1200.B75 2012
 912.73—dc23

                         2011034647

2020 paperback edition ISBN: 978-1-4263-3703-1
2020 library edition ISBN: 978-1-4263-3704-8

Printed in Malaysia
20/IVM/1